Bettina Ratering

SET INTO LIFE

BOOKS on DEMAND

Bettina Ratering

SET INTO LIFE

Bibliografische Information der Deutschen Nationalbibliothek: Die Deutsche Nationalbibliothek verzeichnet diese Publikation in der Deutschen Nationalbibliografie; detaillierte bibliografische Daten sind im Internet über http://dnb.dnb.de abrufbar.

Translation: **Arne Gasch**
Editorial: **Heather David**
Cover Design: **Birgit Spielvogel** www.trend-trade.com
Foto of Child: **Fotolia - Alex Motrenko**
Other contributors: **Amadeus Schmidgall**

Manufactured and published: BoD — Books on Demand, Norderstedt

ISBN: 978-3-7448-3697-5

Preface

This is a very powerful and moving story of a child growing up on the Reeperbahn in Hamburg and of her rescue from that way of life.

In my many years of ministry with Teen Challenge I have, without exaggeration, seen thousands of human lives transformed by God's power.

At the same time I believe that Bettina's life story is one of the most astonishing ones I have read and have myself witnessed.

No one should ever go through such a hell on earth as she did.

Yet, the fact that she is a godly woman today and a leader of the Teen Challenge ministry in Germany, is a testimony for the miracle-performing grace of Jesus Christ.

No one who reads this book should move on and be able to say that God is dead or that Jesus Christ was merely a historical person.

He is alive in Bettina's heart, her mind, her soul and her life, and what Jesus Christ did for her, he can do for everyone.

Don Wilkerson
Founder of Global Teen Challenge

1. Alone

A warm summer breeze was blowing through the streets.

Occasionally, you could hear the sweeping of shards of glass and beverage vehicles picking up the empties from the pubs.

It was silent – almost too silent!

A few hours earlier all hell had broken loose there.

Lights sparkled everywhere, ladies of the night attracted men into the bars.

The sight of women offering themselves and haggling for customers; it wasn't unlike a summer rummage sale, except that here it was womens' bodies for sale!

There were limousines with darkened windows, thugs waiting for their prey, young girls going child-street-walking and being critically observed by their pimps.

And then there were the many people who, out of curiosity just wanted to gape, to have fun.

Mobs of men drawn by the pubs acted out as they never could have done at home.

It was pure unbridled lust for sex and drugs.

The many blinking ads with their oversized nude pictures fired up the emotions and lured customers.

Again and again there was the howling of sirens and police cars flashed past.

Nothing of that sort could be seen now.

What remained was dirt, the stench of alcohol and sweat as well as here and there, a tramp passed out drunk, abandoned, unnoticed.

Such was the daily scene in the David precinct.

Who cared?

Here, everyone was responsible for himself.

This short period of respite in the market of lust and desire was necessary in order to undertake the few personal matters which remained for the people who lived and worked here.

Rosi was sitting at a bar.

The night had left visible traces.

Her face looked like a spilled paint pot.

The applied makeup was heavily smudged and mixed with everything that gave her face colour.

She looked absent, lacking any expression.

She had been here for 2 years.

It felt like an eternity.

And yet, she was only 14 years old, with her life supposedly still ahead of her.

Her parents had chucked her out early from home.

They were both alcoholics and were not able to care for her.

So, she ended up street-walking, to earn some money, although most of her earnings went into the hands of her pimp.

The little that remained for her, was spent on coffee, cigarettes and drugs.

She did not have any fixed abode, and so she slept here or there at a whoremonger's.

Sometimes her pimp, with whom a kind of love-hate relationship had developed over time, took her for himself.

It was a dependency for survival.

He was her protector, dealer, boss and provider.

Apart from her, he had many other girls who had to go hooking for him.

Now, she was alone.

Steam rose from a coffee in front of her and someone behind the counter cleaned up.

In the background you could hear quiet muffled sounds from the radio.

Hastily she poured down the hot contents of the cup.

Rosi stood up and left.

She headed for the port.

She often went there when she was all alone.

Soon, the first tourists, potential customers, would re-emerge, and by then she had to be fit again.

On her way there she made a short detour via a toilet, where she wiped the remaining colour off her face, washed and applied new makeup, styled her long hair and finally set out.

A new day had begun.

2. A Cold Night

Little by little it became more uncomfortable outside.

The warm breeze was replaced by a foggy haze.

That was typical Hamburg weather.

The drizzle permeated the girls' thin clothing as they met in front of the nightclub.

It was 5 pm and not yet the peak period.

Nevertheless, it seemed as if the mile was beginning to bustle.

Rosi was standing surrounded by a crowd of girls all offering their bodies.

She was wearing high-heels, and her mini skirt only just hid the bare essentials.

She rummaged around agitatedly in her purse, once again quickly injecting herself, applying a double layer of lipstick, and now she was ready for the first customer.

It was a battle game between customers, custodians of the law and the girls.

Not one was registered, let alone of legal age – but all were highly sought after.

It was the task of the pimps to protect their goods well, and so they regularly cruised around checking up on their merchandise!

They were to be seen everywhere and yet nowhere.

Rosi froze, trying hard to convince the men passing by with her artificial plastic smile.

Today, she didn't appear to be so convincing.

She couldn't manage to utter any chat-up line.

All she felt, night after night, was an enormous pressure to make money, to supply her need for alcohol and drugs.

Then they came: a group of sex tourists, driven in from somewhere.

With their sharp eyes they were seeking a match for themselves.

And so it happened that even Rosi got her whoremonger, and quickly disappeared with him inside a brothel.

After the obligatory bottle of sparkling wine, she applied the grooming skills in which she had been trained, and then disappeared with him.

Here, it was no problem to rent a room at an hourly rate.

Many even had something resembling a contract with the housekeepers.

Most of them tried to serve as many clients per day as possible, and it also happened that pimps brutally restricted the hours or showed up very quickly with a new potential client.

This happened to Rosi that night.

It was 3am when she, completely run down, resurfaced at the entrance of the nightclub.

Her whole appearance looked much the worse for wear.

A doorman approached her, forcing a kiss on her lips: a sign of power, for otherwise such a kiss was taboo.

Then they settled up.

It was hard business.

In the end, too little remained for her.

Now, she was freezing again.

This time it had not worked out with a warm shelter for the rest of the night.

She got up and trudged along close to the shops and bars, always on the scout.

3. The Offer

Something was wrong.
Rosi felt totally miserable.
"Crap drugs" she thought, as she experienced one emotional outburst after another.
Today she did not even want to see anyone.
The cigarette had no taste.
She had never been seriously ill, and in this industry you simply could not afford to be.
Once she witnessed a girl being brutally beaten up because she had refused to give her services to the pimp.
After a while she stood up again, disappeared into the next toilet, then tripped and staggered towards the night bar.
A man approached her directly, which was very unusual in the mornings.
He looked her up and down, undressing her with his eyes.
He took her wrist and dragged her into a pub.
It was a gambling den.
In the background you could hear men gambling, the shuffling of cards and the smack of billiard shots.
He sat her on a stool, place a glass of beer in front of her and coaxed her to drink.
Then he offered her a joint.
He continued to look at her with his piercing gaze.
A short time passed by and the silence felt like an eternity to Rosi.
What did he want from her?
And what was going on with her boss?
It didn't take long to hear his agenda.
With a haunting gaze and a hoarse voice he started to explain:

"Jan, they got'im! Now you belong to me!" Then he set out the new working conditions.

Rosi was only half-listening.

What had happened to Jan?

Where was the money he still owed her?

Quickly she realized that her new boss wasn't really interested in how she was doing.

He took her into his private area, which was different from what she had previously known..

He paid close attention to ensure that his girls looked good, but when it came to brutality and meanness, he was almost without equal.

He set the prices, had a few rooms upstairs and in part even provided the clientele.

For Rosi this was still no great improvement.

She had to beg him for every drug, and he took full pleasure in hearing her pleas.

She even had almost forgotten her 15th birthday.

However, she started to have an inkling about something appalling ...

After a couple of weeks, she was certain: she was pregnant!

She knew of many who were sent to Holland for an abortion.

She also knew stories where pimps simply had kicked women until they lost their unborn child.

What should she do?

What would happen if she came out?

What would her boss do?

Yes, she was also to blame.

She had been impregnated by some customer.

It was an accident: this was her excuse.

But when and how?

Unfortunately, in this business, pregnancies can't be kept secret for long.

She knew she had to tell him before he found out another way.

She was not even clear about what she wanted or what would happen, and so she was very scared.

Early in the fifth month she seized the right moment for a conversation with her boss.

Drugged to the eyeballs with everything she could get, she went to him and revealed all.

She chose a favourable moment.

Over the last days he had made good money and he was sitting down with her for a glass of beer.

She tried to begin to launch into her explanation again and again,, then all the misery broke loose out of her.

Moments of silence and anxiety ensued.

You could nearly see how he was processing the revelation.

Then came the first reaction: he slapped her across the face.

She began to tremble.

What now?

What would he do to her?

Astonishingly quickly he calmed down and studied her.

Then he began to grin.

"It's a different kind of fun with a pregnant woman. I will get you the right ones." Having said this, he loosed her into the unknown.

It was brutal and degrading.

In spite of her condition, he demanded more and more of her.

Shortly before the delivery she felt so bad, she could hardly breathe.

He allowed her belly to show and she realized that it would not be long until the baby would come.

4. Rosi Seals The Deal

He also seemed to realize, that the pregnancy was almost over.

As if completely changed, he embraced and caressed her, before offering her a room for her private use.

Rosi was allowed to stay there, and only he visited her regularly.

Now, his ambition was clear to her.

He wanted both of them for himself: herself and the baby, and she agreed to it, not that she had much choice!

It was a type of modern slavery, in which she belonged to him, and had no rights.

She was neither registered, nor known to the authorities!

She was only 15 years old!

Her life had, in any case, not belonged to her for a long time.

She had no sense of personal value, nothing, where she could find herself.

She was being determined by the current market value.

For a long time she had realised that even drugs added nothing to improve her life.

She was in fetters, and the ropes were being pulled tighter and tighter.

Without them, she would not be able to hold herself together.

She was imprisoned and without prospects!

Sex, violence and drugs determined the day.

Through the drugs she knew herself to be temporarily in another world, and that made everything else somehow bearable.

The child, that was coming, was annoying just by its existence!

What should she do with it?

She had not even wanted it and she could not make any use of it in her situation.

It would cost time and money.

She was sure that the demands made on her would not be reduced.

It was nothing more than a stupid operational accident.

Almost gratefully she accepted her boss' proposal.

He wanted the child, and he was welcome to it!

She could not and would not assume any responsibility for it.

She herself had not experienced a normal childhood and was hard and without feelings despite being pregnant.

Not even thoughts of murdering the child seemed strange to her.

Only the fear of her boss protected her from doing such a thing.

He visited her very often and his latest trick was to make her dance in front of him until she ran out of breath.

But she simply did not care, because she knew that her situation was a problem of her own doing.

She also knew that this time would come to an end, even if the last few weeks had seemed to be the worst ones.

She almost looked forward excitedly to the day when she would be relieved of this burden.

She wanted to finish the topic "pregnancy and baby" forever.

The baby had to go.

Her boss could do with it what he wanted to.

It never occurred to her that she might want to have something more to do with this child.

5. Pink

Then it was time.

Labour began.

Rosi was trying to let herself be distracted at the bar, but even this no longer helped.

Escape was impossible.

A colleague sat down beside her.

That was good.

She owed it to her that the rear portion of the restaurant was closed, and they retreated there.

In the dark, smoke-filled room was a large pool table.

Evi, as she was called, brought towels from the kitchen and seemed to even know exactly what else would be needed.

Rosi wondered how she knew.

The environment was not a very inviting introduction for a new being.

Rosi neither wanted nor was able to go up to her room.

Her head was spinning.

For the first time, she showed Evi her true emotions.

Tears were in her eyes.

She didn't quite know what was happening.

She only wished that it would be over quickly.

The dark room, the stuffy air and the voices of the bar caused her to sink into depression.

Evi stayed faithfully at her side.

It was comforting to have her there, and at this time of fears and feelings a kind of friendship developed that would continue for a long time.

These were moments marked by the human need for acceptance and love, understanding and support; moments which were almost unknown in Rosi's life, somehow strange, and yet so much longed for.

Never again were the two so closely connected, even though they would be engaged together in the same business many years later.

The contractions came more and more frequently and Rosi began to battle.

Throughout this whole time, the people in the front didn't realise anything about this event.

Any sound was swallowed up by the high noise level.

It took a few hours and then it finally: a baby was born!

Without either a doctor or a midwife, except for the few inside the bar, no one had noticed that it was there.

Evi skilfully clipped the umbilical cord and tended Rosi.

Then she laid the child at Rosi's breast to drink.

It was a girl.

How appropriate, thought Rosi.

She had blue eyes and appeared to be quite healthy at first glance. Her initial feeling of release was quickly replaced by worry creeping in.

What should she do now with this new arrival?

She was neither able nor wanted to breastfeed the baby.

She had never given a thought to choosing a name for the child.

She didn't really belong to her anyway.

Already during the pregnancy she had settled her affairs regarding the child.

Other women who worked there visited her and the girl was named "Heike".

Someone procured everything Rosi needed for baby and helped her with diapering and giving the baby its bottle.

Rosi passed the child across to others more and more.

She did not want it!

Her boss seemed to be thrilled.

He was changed and he treated her with much more consideration.

He made more concessions than before.

Yet, soon he forced her to prostitute again.

The baby had to be sedated.

Rosi started to give sleeping pills to the little one, when she didn't stay quiet.

The crib was placed in her "office".

6. My Mothers

As Heike was handed around so much, she had many mothers.

There was no one who became her real caregiver.

That's the story as it has been told by my mother.

I also learned many things from Evi, and some things about her.

There I was!

Actually, I would also like to have known the "boss".

When I was 4 years old, he had a deadly confrontation with someone, and I could never thank him for telling my mother to carry me to full term.

I only know from hearsay that he softened and had adopted me, so to speak, at least in his heart, if not on paper.

I had no papers, but there were witnesses of my birth, and the women took care of me.

However, the one thing I couldn't do was to get out of this house.

I felt the sun and rain only through the open window.

There was even a will - a handwritten note - which appointed my mother as heir of the bar.

In the meantime she was officially registered in business.

Together with her former colleagues she kept things ticking over.

My mother hired a "housekeeper" an indispensable protector in this situation, whose task was equivalent to that of a pimp.

Gambling operations ceased.

The women had to learn tricks, and my mother became a bitter and hateful boss.

She fixed the prices and toughened the working conditions.

At her side she had a man who protected her in this milieu.

It was a reciprocal dependency arrangement.

She appeared self-confident when she was together with him. .

I think she acted out what she herself had been made to suffer and let others feel that brutality and contempt for humanity.

The girls who worked with her mostly came from troubled and dysfunctional family backgrounds.

Many were from abroad and barely able to communicate.

Often they were very simple and naive and allowed themselves to be ingratiated by young pimps before accepting the offer of prostitution.

The lure of making a lot of money and having enough fun lured them into their fate and misery.

Some were deliberately brought to Hamburg though false promises.

Entire trafficking rings were specialized in leading young women into that modern slavery.

Here, each one fought for themselves.

Profit largely went via the pimp to the head-barkeeper.

The papers of the girls were kept in an inaccessible cupboard in the office.

They were held in complete dependence.

Many were addicted to drugs or had been deliberately lured there.

They lived under the constant pressure of needing dope, which ensured that they remained enslaved and forced to work more, rather than being able to run away.

Those who did not submit to this were threatened with beatings and other forms of torture.

Friendships did not exist.

Only sex, drugs and money counted in this world.

as a result of this there was no one to show me the care I needed.

I received very limited attention because of the pressure forced on to the women.

I was regularly given little treats to keep me quiet.

My mother had the least contact with me, and I soon grew to understand that I was simply an annoyance to her.

From time to time Evi gave me a little time and later she told me that sometimes she had regarded me as her baby.

For a time, it had been her greatest desire to marry and to start a family, but she never came out of that bar.

In 2001 I received the news that, drugged to the eyeballs, she had jumped out of a window.

She died as a result of that fall.

Later, I visited her grave several times while visiting Hamburg.

It has become a memorial for me!

7. Cold And Hot

According to stories I have been told, my real suffering began when I was two years old.

My mother's whoremongers had fun using me as foreplay for their sexual desires, and I was utterly inhumanely abused.

I don't want to go further into this topic.

My mother justified all of that (in a conversation years later) by saying that, after all, I also cost money and in return I should play my part.

Despite this traumatic experience I craved for my mother's care: something I never did receive.

Physical contact was always painful.

So I encapsulated my emotional world in physical numbness for my own self-protection.

Getting older, my movements were still curtailed, and mostly I just hung around with my mother in the room.

I was not allowed to take a look around in the house without express permission.

I was the new (secret) source of income for special customers, and so it had to remain.

They were afraid in case the youth welfare office or any other regulatory agency would become aware of me.

By 4 years of age I was a physical and mental wreck due to the pills I was forced to swallow and the constant abuse I endured, but apparently there was no end in sight.

My mother always emphasized that this was my destiny, and my life would continue in this vein.

Her hatred was boundless, and yet she remained my natural mother, from whom my greatest hope was to receive just one single smile.

For the first time in years, my existence was exposed to the outside world by a drunken patron of the bar.

I owe it to this drunken man, that a Christian organization became aware of me.

With much care and love I was released from my prison.

The attitude and disposition of these people was so different from anything I had experienced before, that I didn't know how to relate.

They were strangers to me.

I was treated kindly and got as much sleep and food as I wanted.

They gave me toys and tried to establish a natural rapport with me, which I found completely overwhelming.

I stayed in this reception centre for 2 weeks.

Legal proceedings were not started against my mother, due to her personal situation.

Today I find that incomprehensible.

Probably there had been hard blows of fate in her life also, which were taken into account by the judges.

That would be the only permissible reason I could understand

8. Inner Strife

Suddenly my new home was many hundreds of kilometres away.

A childrens'home found a foster family for me: a wealthy childless couple.

When I got there, nothing in my state of mind had changed.

I was still numb, unable to cry or laugh.

I winced at any physical touch.

My foster father took pains to help me build a rapport with him.

I still remember him buying a colourful foam cube.

He romped and tumbled over it with me, and through this, I finally began to smile.

It was the beginning – how much I loved laughing later.

But it was not easy to slip from one world to the other.

It was quite a culture shock.

Speaking took even longer. The first words I uttered clearly were "car" and "plane".

"A child of the 20th century", reasoned my foster mother, who would have preferred me to have said "mom".

But I could not.

The inner longing for my mother remained. Anyway, the relationship with my new parents was rather a mutual arrangement based on using one another and convenience, in particular as far as it concerned my foster mother.

She could not have children but wanted one, although if truth be known, actually she would have preferred a boy.

I needed care and education, which my real home had denied me.

Here, I got everything.

Materially nothing was lacking.

I was nurtured so that I could keep up the standards of a family of academics.

My foster mother was a pharmacist and my father was a mining assessor.

They were at home in the upper crust and their household was structured accordingly.

Cultural and high societal interaction were not lacking.

One used the cutlery from the outside inwards.

One had to follow the etiquette manual, and as a child one remained silent at the table.

One was well and neatly dressed, and had to curtsey when visitors came.

As the daughter of the house I had to meet a certain standard.

Today I am reminded a bit of the story of Moses, who came from a family of slaves into the house of Pharaoh.

I had moved from the swamps of Reeperbahn to a solid, well-educated and wealthy home.

The only thing that really was missing was a love relationship.

I wasn't able to express love, and my foster family was unable to give it to me.

I loved my mother above everything and no other woman could compensate.

I did not even want to allow anyone to get in between this relationship.

They could try as hard as they wanted.

There she was, the little rebel inside me.

No matter what other changes I had to accept, I would not give up my relationship with my mother!

That was deep down inside me.

Just like the idea that these new parents envisioned for themselves, which they did not deserve.

But at this time I was still too small to actively oppose them.

9. Who Are You?

I asked myself this question when I was very young Everything that reminded of my old home, was taken from me.

The most far-reaching change was the change of name.

Suddenly, I was "Bettina" instead of "Heike", because they liked this name better, and with it my mother's family name was erased.

I was given a birthday, on which day my birth was celebrated.

As a matter of course a candle wreath was set up with the determined years, and it was said that on this day I would be e.g. 7 years old.

What nonsense!

Even to this day I am not so much into celebrating birthdays, although I do affirm my life.

Then came the day of school enrolment.

Everything was changed, none of the data entered bore any truth.

My foster parents truly tried hard to give me a new identity.

In the neighbourhood they said that I had been adopted from a home, and so I had to be given a new family name.

I suffered a lot because of it, but I didn't defend myself at that time.

Who I really was, slipped more and more out of my control.

What I kept were my inner pictures, and I kept them like a precious treasure.

In my dreams I often slipped back to Hamburg; the house, the bar, everything was alive again.

But the terrible pain returned and I started to sleep-walk.

Quite often in the morning, my foster mother retrieved me, rolled up in the wall cabinet.

All medical examinations to identify the cause were unsuccessful.

For years I had wild nightmares with ever-repeating pictures and situations.

Today, I can still relive one picture.

It was the clicking of a revolver trigger and the sensation of a cold barrel at my temple.

Often, I would scream and wake up drenched in sweat.

I even started bed-wetting, which led my foster mother, as a pharmacist, to give me something against cystitis, which of course did not help.

Due to my psychological challenges I was ill many times.

My immune system was very weak and so I suffered with associated conditions such as asthma and allergies, including neurodermatitis

My body was like a crumbly cake.

From the medical side everything had been tried, but my soul and consequently my mental state remained ill.

There are pictures that show me sitting in the bathtub with bandaged arms, so I wouldn't begin to scratch open the sores on my arms.

I had every treatment possible but with very little success.

I was often sick, especially in the early years.

10. The Friends

Within the new family I was by far the youngest as there were no other children.

Thus family celebrations turned out to be rather boring.

I had to behave like an adult, not playing, and conversations were always highly scientific or political.

Now and then I was presented to recite a poem or play something on the flute or the piano.

It was absolutely terrible.

Because of this I was jolly glad when a couple of kids moved into our neighbourhood, and I could be excused every once in a while.

They were all boys.

One went to school with me, and we had many adventures together.

So I played soccer, built slot car racing tracks, conquered one or another climbing tree and examined abandoned buildings: all those things which girls, in the eyes of my family, do not do.

We also went to the police and claimed to have seen a drowned body in our town lake.

The report was received, and we drove to the lake in a police car.

The whole thing turned out to be children's imagination.

Yet, the consequence was that my foster parents threatened I would be sent to prison because of this tall tale.

I was terrified and had to stay in my room for the rest of the day, waiting to be picked up by the police.

My foster mother came from the Berg and Upper Land of Berg.

A few of her relatives lived here and thus regular visiting tours were made.

In a dear aunt's neighbourhood there was a farm with many children: six girls and one boy.

I made a particularly quick connection to the boy, as we were of the same age.

I began to love the adventure of countryside and farm.

Yes, I loved to go there, although I did not like the long and sometimes fast car drive at all.

I often felt sick as my foster father had the habit of smoking a pipe during the drive.

The rural life did good for me.

I fed the animals, liked to smell the fresh grass in the silo, and picked up the fresh milk in the evenings.

Always, when I had seemingly got lost, I was to be found in the barn.

When the cows were brought in from the pasture in the evening, I always had to be there.

From a distance I called out to them and tried to beckon them to the exit.

I had a special relationship with animals and had the feeling that they understood me.

In the cow barn there was one black cow among all the brown and white ones.

Not only the colour, but the whole animal was different and assumed a special position within the herd.

It had grown particularly close to my heart.

I thought of it as an outsider, maybe as little understood as I was, and I told it everything I was dealing with.

It was a little oasis, and there we cherished a mutual treasure.

I had another contact with a dear senior lady, who was a former teacher and knew how to engage me in conversation.

Besides the big house on a hillock she had wood and pastures on which were small ponies.

We both fed the animals with potato and apple peel, and she told me a lot about how to keep animals and how the animals had come there.

Each one had its own story and I could listen for hours.

But the best part was, she had a little wire-haired dachshund.

I loved that dog, and whenever I was there, I took time for long strolls with this animal through the woods and meadows.

It was the time when my ideas and also my dream world came thick and fast, and I longed to find myself.

I could sit by the brook, watching the little dachshund for hours, as he followed his hunting instinct.

He was called "Falk" and I had a closer relationship with him than with any other creature around me at that time.

When the little dog died, the value of these visits changed.

One day I borrowed a child's bike from the farm, where the many children lived.

I cycled back and forth across the landscape. In the end I left the bike somewhere, and afterwards I forgot where.

That brought massive trouble and I had to give them my own bike from home, to replace the missing one.

Nobody explained why to me, and I was very sad.

In school, I didn't relate with my fellow classmates. After all, except for that neighbourhood friendship, I rather assumed a role as an outsider.

My performance was rather mediocre, and basically I was one of the slow ones as far as learning was concerned.

My afternoons consisted of homework, tutoring, music lessons, and there was hardly any time to play.

When I was nine years old I joined a choir with my foster parents and sang in the first soprano section.

I liked to do that, because we were never home before 10 pm.

The riding stable was one of the big highlights of that period.

As a gift for my 8th birthday I was given riding lessons at a classy riding club, with which my foster father had a particularly good relationship.

They made sure that I was as good as possible and could participate in my first small competitions.

Everything was about performance, never just for the fun of it.

When I was thirteen years old I developed a horse dust allergy and the issue was settled.

Overall, I grew up in a world shaped by adults.

Today I like playing Playmobil with my kids or dressing up in something crazy.

I enjoy it when my children invite friends and the farm is alive with children's voices.

I take pleasure in them and joyfully take in this atmosphere.

What could be better than jumping boisterously and happily around without being burdened by all the seriousness and oppression in the world, and rushed by work and time?!

Children can do this, if you let them!

And as an adult it feels so good to slip into this children's world.

11. Without Sound

I do not remember exactly when it was, that I started to become rebellious.

When my foster parents were out, I searched the cupboards.

Actually I was looking for myself when I came across some things from former times: papers, photographs, names.

In doing so I also opened the cupboard where my foster father had his tobacco
and kept his cigarettes.

I secretly began to smoke.

As my father was a smoker himself, it didn't attract any attention when I smoked in the house.

What's more, the liquors in the basement started to win my attention.

It started with a bottle of beer ... The basement was equipped with a wide range of liqueurs, wine, schnapps and beer.

My foster father liked to drink, and when he was out with his folks, or at the "Crackerbarrel", he often came home drunk.

But that was legal and above board.

Once I found and emptied a whole bottle with leavened in the cellar and then had to be hospitalized.

It was the first time that my foster parents really punished me, and I had to accept weeks of house arrest.

Meanwhile, they gave flowers and tried to apologize for my wrongdoings to their family doctor.

They had to save face.

But I fought back and began to steal, even though I could have had anything without stealing.

I wanted to show clearly that I was against them.

I was me and not their sweet, well-behaved girl who socialised so maturely with adults.

Drunkenness, tablets and hospital stays occurred more and more regularly.

Totally unconscious, I was brought to the emergency room by people who knew me.

As they pushed me in a wheelchair for examination, I leaned over and fell to the floor.

When the nursing staff tried to help me, I began to kick and beat them.

That evening ended with me being strapped in bed.

For my foster parents, the situation was becoming more and more embarrassing.

Crazed behaviour at the hospital was a visible cry for help, but no one knew how to deal with me.

12. The Boy In Our Neighbourhood

Right next to us lived a boy, who was 17 years old and already doing an apprenticeship.

He loved turning up his stereo system to aggravate the neighbours with his noise.

I admired him because he did what I would have liked to do as well.

So I clung to him and visited him regularly in his digs.

He became my great role model of independence and strength.

His parents seemed to simply leave him alone.

When they wanted something from him, he shouted at them as they came into his room and booted them out.

People smoked in his room and sometimes he smoked a joint.

As a little girl I was very proud of having such a big friend.

He regularly picked me up from school on his scooter, and I boasted about it in class.

One day I didn't go to him straightaway, but rather, moved on walking a short distance around the city lake.

He took me firmly by the hand and then I got my first kiss from him.

I found it disgusting, but I didn't say anything and just let it happen.

He came right up to me with increasing regularity and then he asked me to sleep with him.

He pulled me into the thick clusters of bushes and I let everything wash over me like a doll.

It was as if my nervous system was paralysed.

After this experience all the memories came back at once.

My mother, Hamburg ... - and I felt like a discarded, used handkerchief being sniffed back inside the nose.

I retained this image for a long time.

Then there was the usual fearmongering advice which, however, did not impress me.

Nevertheless I kept contact with him, but never again did it come to an unwanted assault.

A pattern of co-dependency developed between us.

I was totally submissively dependent on him, and his gaze was enough to direct me.

Often we were in his gaff, smoking pot together and we had sex time and again.

However, I was so stimulated by it, that I did not care, what he did to me.

My parents didn't realise what was happening there until I moved out.

They had simply advised me to stay away from the boy as they didn't find him a good influence on me.

By this time – I do not know if it was through all the drugs I had consumed – I had developed a violent temper.

I had these outbursts very often while I was taking drugs and so it was that there were shards of glass shattering or doors were tested for their stability.

The temper outbursts were uncontrollable, but always short.

Afterwards, I mostly felt sorry, especially when my own stuff suffered as a result.

13. School

In 6th grade, I realized that I could get through just fine without much effort.

I got along very well with my teachers and due to my class participation I was also popular with my classmates.

The lessons never got boring, as I again and again brought in a casual interlude and triggered discussions.

But behind it was a lot of rebellion, wanting to be different from others.

For the most part I did my homework in school.

My foster parents couldn't keep up with me, so they didn't even realise, whenever I skipped classes and disappeared in the town's pub.

It wasn't just an alternative club, in which the chosen dropouts of the town used to meet up, it was also where heavy drugs were dealt.

Since I always had enough cash from home (my allowance was unreasonably high), I regularly bought a few grams of hashish.

I belonged among them, which was very important to me!

However, the more I started to use drugs, the more aggressive I became.

In school, my performance worsened and I got my first bad grades in my report.

I began to engage in fights in school, and I even bloodied a boy who had used my volleyball as a football, which resulted in me being suspended from school for one day.

I had a feasible explanation for my foster parents. After all I was becoming more and more cunning in my racketeering and statements.

I never worried if I would be moved up to the next class, and so school became a lesser evil which I simply had to accept.

But sometimes I enjoyed the school environment as it also offered some variety which I was looking for.

It was fun to distract my teachers.

14. Not Too Close

"Keep off my pitch" became the standard phrase with which I could keep most people in the pub at bay.

When I was crabby, I lifted up one end of the table and let the beer glasses "accidentally" tumble to the ground.

I wore spiky rivetted bracelets on my arms, and around my waist dangled a chain as a belt, which at a pinch I could also use as a weapon.

However, it wasn't just that I saw others as enemies: I simply found it fun to beat others.

In my town I had discredited myself among the youth – and I enjoyed being different, even if it made me an outsider again.

Besides the usual rivetted bracelets and skin-tight jeans I also wore loose-fitting miners' shirts fastened with an oversized safety pin which you could find in the changing room of the coal mines.

I changed my hairstyle as the fancy took me: from long to short, dyed or natural, just as it suited me.

Washing was totally uncool and so I walked around in the same clothes for weeks.

When my foster mother dared to wash an item of clothing without my permission, she received a fiery response.

I think at that point my foster parents realised they were overwhelmed with trying to parent me.

I had the feeling they didn't understand anything.

For example, my father asked me really seriously if I would like to go to an opera with them, after I had declared war on any classical music!!! Actually, I had the feeling I was from another planet.

15. Church

My foster parents attended the protestant church. There, they had their roles which they took very seriously.

Both sang in the choir, which I had left at the age of 12.

As a child, I had to go to church every Sunday morning, although they remained at home to accomplish more important things.

Church would not hurt me, they thought, however, I was not interested in that at all.

So, after the first song I went out with all the kids and then, instead of marching faithfully to the parish hall, I walked to the cinema.

It was an old cinema, and I could often get admitted through the back door.

I loved watching x-rated movies the most.

I even watched horror movies, like "The Exorcist", "Jaws", etc. As a late sequel to these cinema visits I still have problems swimming in the sea or in swimming pools up to this day!

Later, at the age of 13, I seriously contemplated God.

I had to go to confirmation classes, and I was confirmed at the age of 14.

Even here I bandied blows in front of the parish hall, which rather amused our pastor.

He told my parents how well I could hold my own against the cheeky boys. Yes, he regarded everything very positively and even said how strong I was.

At that time I also went on a retreat in Austria with a youth group, though I was more interested in the guys and cigarettes.

I heard much about Jesus during that time, but it didn't go down well with me.

There was a devotion every day, and most of the participants supported what the leaders shared.

It became an almost legalistic rule that one should read from the Bible every day.

Pious crazy ideas! I belonged to a different group.

Nevertheless, I believe that God may have planted a seed there.

In fact, as a confirmand I even co-supervised the children's Sunday School for one year.

That was better than sitting through a dry church service and it was also fun to teach the kids, to tell some nice stories and leave them believing that everything said in the church is true.

I wasn't involved in that church, in any other way, and I left it without being challenged by the Gospel. As a co-worker in the children's ministry, I had the keys to the parish hall, which I used for my own private purposes.

So I regularly met with some buddies and we calmly smoked and drank a few beers together.

At that time, the building was still smoker-friendly.

Even the worship leader always walked around the building with a pipe in his mouth.

He felt it was quite normal for us to be there and his son often joined us.

He was the same age as me, and we knew each other from the choir.

Even he was rebellious towards his family and was trying to opt out of the good middle-class life.

However, over time his family influenced him, and in my eyes he did a U-turn.

Through school and confirmation classes, I also came to know a girl who came from a broken home but lived in a huge mansion with her father.

He was a photographer and had a studio with a photo lab set up in the house.

The girl, who was also named Bettina, had half of the house for herself.

She could come and go as she pleased, and no one really minded.

Her old grandma, an alcoholic, lived in a room in the same hallway, and she was sometimes very stressful.

She drank and smoked, and it reeked like a pub.

My new friend was able to handle that well, and she ignored it whenever possible.

From time to time, she also cooked for her grandma and me.

I loved to milk her liberty for myself.

I often visited her so I could smoke in peace and rest from all the stress in town and at home.

A small park was next to the villa, and I often used to camp in my tent when I didn't want to go home.

It was pure freedom for me.

My friend did not always understand my behaviour, but she was an outsider like me, and that bound us together.

16. Trouble

At 14 I totally freaked out. Whereas in the beginning, I had only tested and pushed the limits, I was now well over any limit.

So, I often pretended to stay overnight with friends from school, while actually I was wandering through the town at night.

Smoking weed was no longer enough for me: I needed something stronger.

So I mixed pills and alcohol, and consequently was taken to hospital several times to have my stomach pumped.

I went deeper and deeper into the swamp of lies linked with alcohol and drugs.

More and more I was looking for my own kind of freedom, detached from all social norms.

My foster parents certainly still tried to help me, but I declined all help.

When they made an appointment at the counselling centre, I made sure on principle that I was not there.

When they locked me in to protect me, I jumped out of the window.

They tried coaxing and sanctions but they couldn't get through to me any longer.

Then the police brought me home, because once again I had attracted attention.

It all escalated.

I questioned everything.

I challenged their right to behave as my parents and asserted that my time at home was over.

I was hurtful and brutal in the way I treated them.

More and more we kept out of each others' way.

We only exchanged words if it was absolutely essential and I promised them I would finish school.

Our relationship was as good as dead.

More and more I leaned towards people from my scene, where I sought community and comfort.

We all had the same goal: opt out of this over-regulated society.

We really felt clever and detached. In our confusion we tore our "stuffy old men" to shreds.

17. First Contact

The town pub, with all the freaky people of the Hard Rock music scene became my new home and the constant police raids belonged to it.

Before school, after school and with increasing frequency I would be found there.

And then, the step to hard drugs was no longer far off.

My first experience with heroin was when I was 15 years old.

It was my birthday party.

It was given to me, and it was an exciting moment.

I was free like a bird.

I enjoyed floating to the music and forgot everything around me.

I did not want to lose this feeling!

But I did, sooner than I had expected, and I got really sick!

There it was, the demand, the urgency.

I smoked a joint, then swallowed some pills, and believed I could survive the school day.

It was no secret that I had drug problems, but yet again, the drug-czar teacher took me out of class and tried to appeal to my conscience.

He offered to accompany me to drug counselling and threatened to write home.

That left me cold.

In the afternoon I was back in the pub to hang out. It was my second home.

18. Friend Or Foe

Sometimes, even weirdos came into this pub.

There was, for example, a group of pious fools who tried to talk to people about the meaning of life, even though it was pointless.

The only thing that still mattered was to make your own life as comfortable as possible.

As I am someone keen to debate and loved to provoke people, their pub outreaches often were an interesting distraction for me.

It became something like a love-hate relationship with these people.

When I could make use of them, I showed an interest in them and pretended to agree with their ideas about faith.

But often I stonewalled and mocked them good and proper!

Sometimes I even used them as a cover for my criminal activities.

So I palmed a stolen bike off on them, as I wanted to get rid of it by any means.

Quite often I also arrived at a young woman's apartment and asked for a place to sleep, when I did not want to go home on "a high."

As a reward for their "good deeds" I once visited their youth meetings.

They invited me to a youth choir, which I attended from time to time, because for me singing was generally fun, and I had a well-trained voice due to my choir days.

But actually I couldn't care less about that:I just wanted to savour the benefits.

And yet, I know now that God was also already working at that point.

Despite all my stubborn opposition some seed fell on fertile ground.

Having been trained as a soprano singer in the choir, I even performed with a youth bible choir.

Singing was still fun for me, even if content wise I could not and did not want to get involved with the songs.

It was all about "ME"

Sometimes I wondered why I went, but somehow it had its charm.

My foster parents found this approach more appealing than the rest of my contacts, even though for me it remained a game I played with people and their feelings.

I would not let anyone touch the real me.

19. I Don´t Care!

I clearly remember dutifully sitting at home at Easter, eating the special dinner and listening to my foster father.

Seemingly he had concrete thoughts about my future.

He was thinking of A levels, university study or a practical apprenticeship.

My foster mother would have preferred me to be a nurse.

It was all planned out for me, but no one asked me what I wanted.

I was outraged, how they were planning my life.

Did they not see that they were out of touch with me, and had been for years?

They simply rode roughshod over me, although I was sitting at the same table.

I had promised to finish school, but I finished after the 10th grade.

I had never thought of doing the senior grades or a high-school diploma.

I was not one of the nerds.

For me, school was rather annoying and I had absolutely no desire to stay for a further 3 years.

And not only that, it would also have meant that I would still have had to live three more years in this house.

That was unthinkable!

I battened down the hatches within myself.

As my opinion was not even asked, I stood up and went to my room.

Alongside many horse postcards there were posters of Udo Lindenberg on my walls.

In those days, I found him cool.

Not only that, but Rocky was with him on his concerts.

He was totally wicked, having perfected the art of opting out.

Why couldn't I do that?

What do I care for my foster parents, who only have their own plans in mind?

It isn't really about me anyway.

Couldn't they get their heads around it that I was completely different than they thought?

By no means was I going to live a conventional life!

I would boogie soon enough.

The decision was made and I felt exhilarated.

Cheered by my new resolution I once again trotted off to town.

I passed a petrol station and bought, in addition to the usual cigarettes and beer reserves, a map of Hamburg as well.

Even at Easter our pub was open all day and night.

I sat down at an empty table, rolled a fat joint for myself and spread out the city map.

My eyes were fixed on St. Pauli, as hat was where I was from.

I wanted to go back there.

As if drawn by a magnet, my eyes focussed on the area around the Reeperbahn.

Something like a sense of homesickness arose in me while I was drinking the third
beer.

How was my mother doing?

Slowly I began dreaming and painting everything in the finest images.

I could have sunk into those thoughts forever.

In contrast, everything else seemed bleak and outdated.

I knew my time here was up and I would never even set foot in this pub again.

I would miss some of the people but I could invite them all to Hamburg.

Probably, it would be even better for acquiring dope.

Here it had often been so cumbersome to make a detour across the border, although the thrill also had its appeal. Inwardly I said goodbye to this town.

In the evening I went to Peter and found him going through cold turkey.

I promised to get him something as he was one of my pub group, who was not very well.

Strictly speaking I had known him since the Christian retreat in Austria.

I knew that he, unlike me, wanted more than just a casual friendship.

He had withdrawn from drugs once, but didn't stick it out properly.

Together with him I had got into the drug scene, but I was convinced that I would not end up like him.

Often he overdid it, setting his dose very high.

Now he had no money left and did anything to get dope.

I had no worries on that score, because thanks to my foster parents, I never had money problems.

I came home late at night.

My parents had gone to a concert.

First I wanted to hang up the Hamburg map, but I didn't.

Where I disappeared was none of their business.

That was my secret.

20. Teacher's Conference

It was just before the summer holidays.
The beautiful weather distracted me from learning even more than usual.

I enjoyed hanging around town and enjoying the warm days.

Since deciding to bring my time came here to an end, I had not made much effort in school.

The school, however, was not so tolerant, and so it was that a class conference was convened.

My school absence days had increased substantially and whenever I was present, I disturbed class so much, according to the teacher, that it was questionable if it still made sense to keep me there.

My parents had to come to school.

I had the impression they were flabbergasted, but they managed to find a way for me to stay.

However, I had to accept some significant constraints.

I sensed that I should clean up my act for these few weeks and try to graduate since that was what I had promised.

So the last weeks were very calm and balanced.

Even though it was hard for me, I tried to attend classes regularly.

Inwardly, I was very, very distant, but I was also motivated because I wanted to bring school to a successful finish.

This one thing was important to me.

Actually, it was fun for me to flex my brain cells.

I knew I could compete with the cleverest ones when I did my best.

Whereas others had to work for weeks I grasped new subject matter quickly and applied it within a few days.

So again I caught up in in a very short time.

My certificate was okay and this also gave me a sense of serenity.

In my mind it was all secondary.

The main thing was that I had done it and had concluded this chapter for myself.

There was a graduation party with the teachers.

I went, but I was only interested in the alcohol and whatever else belongs to a party.

Despite my many difficulties I had a rather good relationship with the class teacher.

I talked with him about my plans for the future, which I conjured up from my imagination!

They had little to do with reality.

My goal was Hamburg.

21. Going Home

There it was, the long awaited day!
Everything went according to the usual routine.

Getting up, getting dressed, I even tidied up my room and made my bed.

Then I looked around once more.

I had lived here for so many years.

Memories came to mind and even something like mourning surfaced.

It was not as easy to leave as I had expected!

I wondered briefly if I should take something, but I didn't.

In Hamburg I wouldn't need anything, as my mother was there.

I went for breakfast.

Although I usually wouldn't be able to swallow a morcel at that early hour, on that day I really tucked in.

It was the last time that my foster mother would make me a hot cocoa and a school sandwich, which she wrapped up for me.

This time I was grateful to her for it.

The journey would take a long time and it was good to have a few provisions.

It was a scant goodbye; I couldn't manage more.

My foster father had already gone to work.

I would have liked to say goodbye to him.

My communication channel with him was much better than with my mother.

I looked around one last time and then shut the door.

I headed towards school and picked up my school certificate, before taking the bus to the train station.

I left behind my remaining school things and didn't take anything other than what I was wearing plus some money for the journey.

I managed to catch a connecting train; a half day trip and I would arrive in my hometown.

I deliberately held on to my first impressions.

This was my city!

I headed to Reeperbahn on the S1, but first I took quite a ride through the city.

I was touched.

Whatever it was that was happening inside me, it had to do with the deep desire to finally come home.

22. The Disappointment

Just arrived!

Having got out of the train at the station, I needed to orientate myself as I had never been here.

Where did I have to go anyway?

I should find the street first.

Searching, my gaze wandered from one bar to another.

There had to be something that I still recognised.

Everything looked very outlandish to me.

I had never seen so many adult entertainment services in one place.

Excited and yet confident, I progressed towards the end of the Mile.

I returned along the opposite side.

Then my eyes were caught by a flashing red sign.

That must be it.

Bouncers were standing at the entrance.

In the window all the deals offered in this bar were listed.

How could I go in there?

I stayed in the vicinity of the entrance for about an hour, smoking one cigarette after another.

All sorts of things went through my head.

Will I recognize my mother?

How do I look?

What will I tell her?

I began to formulate an opening line and then I rejected it again.

I pictured my mother, happily surprised, running towards me and hugging me.

Well, she couldn't help but be happy to finally have me back.

A reunion of mother and daughter.

I painted that picture for myself in full colour.

But first I had to get in there and that seemed to be my biggest challenge.

The bouncers were still there and did not look as if they would let me in.

Then I got the great idea of simply asking for my mother.

Surely they would know her name.

So I took my courage in both hands, with my heart in my mouth.

Amazingly, the man I asked did not really listen, but pointed towards the entrance and gruffly told me to enter.

I had not imagined it to be so easy!

There were flashing lights everywhere, it was very dark and my eyes had to get used to the dim lighting.

A desk was on the left side.

There were a few women waiting for customers.

Where should I look for my mother?

I felt lost and sensed I was being viewed with suspicion.

Dressed as I was, I didn't belong here.

It became embarrassing.

A woman turned to me and looked at me critically.

She asked if I had lost my way.

There was giggling behind the counter.

I just wanted to shrivel up.

Suddenly, a skinny woman entered the room from a back room.

She came right up to me and asked what I wanted.

She didn't look as if she was fully in her right senses, and being a connoisseur of the scene I immediately knew she had taken something.

First, I lacked words, then I asked for my mother.

Now I had all the attention.

The woman looked at me intently and asked who had sent me.

Then I burst out: "You are my mother!"

The woman composedly took me by the wrist, drawing me backwards.

"What do you want from me?" she snapped at me, with her eyes suddenly looking mad – yes - eyes which became filled with hatred.

"Get lost!" she screamed.

Aghast, I stared at her.

I had not envisioned our reunion to be like that!

I had come here to live with my mother.

What should I do now?

Why had she reacted so strongly?

I somehow tried to put my helplessness into words.

She evaded me, blocked me.

She clearly made me understand that I had to go.

Yet, suddenly she handed me a blue banknote (100 DM) as if considering whether she would have work for me. She pushed me out.

23. I Need You

Back on the street, I was dazzled by the sun. Still feeling dazed, I headed for the nearest pub.

With the money still in my hand, I sat down at the counter.

A man, half drunk, tried to mack on me from the side.

It was all the same to me.

I ordered a beer and felt that I desperately needed dope now.

Here, I didn't know the ropes. I needed to look for guys who were on dope and could help me, which worked out.

It was summer and thus the days were long, bright and warm.

But night came and I knew I was now living on the street.

Somehow, clumsily, I looked for a night's lodging in a house alcove.

The disappointment ran deep.

Never in my life would I have expected such an encounter.

If I had learned to cry, it would have been much easier to bear, but I could not.

What should I do now?

I wouldn't be willing to go back, even if I was paid.

The first night was very uncomfortable.

I had nothing apart from my jacket, which served as a cushion and covering.

I needed my mother.

I had been waiting to be with her for so many years.

I wandered around the area from 3am onwards.

Where and how should I live now?

What could my mother offer me as work?

Did she think that I wanted to sell my body?

Didn't she know who I was? - Me, who always got everything I needed!

But I wasn't there any longer ... She should help me!

Even if she did not want me, she could at least give me some advice about where I could stay here.

By now it was six o'clock in the morning, and I saw someone cleaning up in a bar.

I asked for a coffee and sat down.

The man, who had let me in, served me.

It was the first time someone spoke kindly to me.

He wanted to know a lot about me, but I was careful: who knows – maybe I was already "wanted" here.

My only thought was: I needed my mother in order at least to be able to live here legally.

24. Street-Walking

The day seemed to dawn slowly.
Everywhere was filthy as the street sweeper swept the shards out of the gutter.

A cold reeking smell emanated from the bars.

A fast food restaurant was offering breakfast, and I remembered I still had a last bit of cash.

I wanted to have another try with my mother.

So I heading off there, only to find everything was still locked up.

But at the side there was a gate, through which I came into the back yard.

A door stood open, revealing a stairwell, which I entered.

Slowly, I went upstairs and found the rooms of the barmaids on the second floor.

On the third floor was a parlour, and behind it seemed to be another living area.

I heard noises and found her.

My mother looked very harassed.

Even with her, night seemed to have left traces.

I saw here inhaling something as I entered.

She looked at me stroppily without saying anything.

I found a seat and waited, until suddenly she poured each of us a glass of booze and sat down.

Without looking at me, she suggested I could work in the strip bar.

No! I realized how uncomfortably that suggestion made me feel. I didn't want that.

A dialogue, which I will never forget, followed.

She told me all that she had been through with me; how much time and money I had cost; that I had not given enough in return and eventually was also taken away from her.

My destiny was to be a streetwalker for money, and this is what I should gear myself up for.

She'd already set up the right guys for me.

She had a financial manager in the business, to whom she entrusted all the transactions.

This also included the whoremongers, of which one should be assigned to me.

When she was finished, I couldn't think or say anything.

I felt I had wronged her and had the feeling that I had to make good again.

Maybe she would love me then.

I did want that.

To gain her love I would even be willing to work for her, even though I had never done such a thing.

I suggested to rather work in the bar.

But she outfitted me and sent me to the street to find customers.

In return, I had to hand in my earnings.

I always tried to secretly withhold money because I needed it to be able to push away all the perverse men, but I had to play along.

However, I didn't always get away with keeping back money.

When I was caught, I was struck with a black belt.

I felt terrible physically and had to be careful not to vomit when I once again had a total pervert in front of me.

I began to despise humans, as I saw only brokenness around me.

I lost my own personality as my feelings dulled more and more, until finally I became ice cold.

When I saw men, I only felt scorn; I only saw the dirt.

At the very top: money was king: it was about nothing else.

I got less and less sleep.

I felt as if I was on the assembly line, where one shift chased the next.

My mother didn't care that my physical and mental condition was deteriorating.

25. The Acquaintance

After a few days a young pimp from another brothel came to me.

He hoped to poach me, which was not without its dangers.

He was one of the brutal ones, one of those who was the first to give up his role of safeguarding.

He wanted me, but I fled.

I ran.

"If I don't fancy him, then I am dead", I thought.

I took refuge with a friend who had absolutely no connection with that sex scene.

He was a drug addict and a burglar, who made money through receiving and handling stolen goods.

I could recharge in his home and it felt almost like a holiday.

I did not go out of my hiding place, but of course, I did not trust this place of asylum either.

If he needed money, he would squeal on me, I knew.

I was still too close to the red-light district.

Being mentally rock-bottom, I was increasingly overcome by a deep depression.

What should I do?

I tried to find support, but nothing gave me real fulfilment, or could satisfy my deeply hidden longing.

Not even drugs helped.

After a week, I couldn't take it any longer.

I had to get out for some fresh air.

Cautiously and anxiously, I moved along the house walls, always panicking that someone might recognize me.

In addition, my appearance was not exactly helpful.

So I borrowed clothes from an acquaintance.

I definitely looked very unusual, because not everything fitted, but I didn't care.

I dyed my hair and got myself a pair of glasses.

In spite of all this effort I was still living in fear.

I could not stay here any longer; I had no money and I was living on credit.

I solemnly promised to settle everything.

26. The Salvation Army

During one of my short outings in the area I met a group of Christians wearing uniforms.

They stood together singing old church hymns, of which I knew none.

Did they have no self-respect with their ridiculous performance!

Who wanted to hear that?

However, even so, I stood still for a moment.

They had a standard bearer and it all looked a bit funny, reminding me of both carnival and circus at the same time.

They were from the Salvation Army.

I knew they had a tea room in the Valley Road, with the words "Jesus in St. Pauli" above the entrance.

In my eyes they were mega religious weirdos, although you could pick up some free tea and sandwiches there. Everything was offered freely, and in exchange we were supposed to listen to their pious lines.

They also had a clothing store, where I could possibly obtain some appropriate clothes.

They belonged to the neighbourhood and were widely ridiculed, tolerated and accepted because of their social vein.

Yes, actually they were sweet and not anxious to cheat us.

And yet I had the feeling that they wanted to sell us their faith in exchange for us ordering a hot tea.

I thought how it would look, if I kicked around the area in such a uniform.

First, I would cut everyone down to size until they believed my ideology.

Despite the seriousness of my situation, I had to smile.

Good thing, I was not so cheap to buy!

I went ahead, holding on to this crazy image.

In the end, I went further along the Valley Road and then back to my hiding place.

I decided to sneak in to the Salvation Army in the following days, thinking it would be good to have some new rags.

However, I still had my pride, and was growing more and more afraid.

I knew that my running away and hiding would get found out sooner or later.

I was ready to go far away; I couldn't stand things the way there were any longer.

27. Let's Scram

After obtaining new trousers and t-shirts, I planned my escape route.

My acquaintance had told me a lot about Zurich, and I had become curious.

He obviously had contacts in Niederdorf, the drug scene of that city, and was willing to give me an address.

But first I had to get out of here unnoticed.

I ran up to the Landing Bridge and took the commuter train out of town to the end station.

From there I hitch-hiked everywhere.

In order to have some money, I offered my body in between stops.

I lied to the last truck driver before the border, telling him some kind of pitiful story so that he would smuggle me through.

Then I was in Switzerland.

I made a stopover in Basel, where I enjoyed the warm weather and let my feet dangle in the Rhine.

I was completely relaxed and holiday mood had taken over.

Basel, I quickly realized, was a very expensive place.

No matter what I wanted to buy, it cost me a fortune.

So I began to organize my shopping rather illegally.

I stayed a week in town and camped under the bridge across the Rhine.

Here there was a whole lot of bustle at night.

There were many hitchhikers and city strollers alike, who spent their nights under the cover of the bridge.

Again, I found good opportunities to act and work.

Had my goal not been different, I could have adopted Basel as my new home.

One day I grabbed my stuff and went to the highway, where I was picked up by a lorry driver. From there we went directly to Zurich.

The address I had obtained in Hamburg was wrong.

This immediately triggered frustration and disappointment; I felt very alone and helpless.

The houses and narrow alleys looked a bit run down, but otherwise Niederdorf gave a rather peaceful impression.

For me, it was not at all comparable to the Reeperbahn.

However, there were other junkies loitering everywhere, and the sight of them hanging out was typical in this area.

Deer Square (Hirschplatz) was the centre for all the action.

Street musicians and artists of all kinds performed to earn some money.

Drug addicts loitered backstage and many prostitutes hung around at the corners.

For me all that took time to get used to.

I didn't know anybody here, and I lacked any orientation.

I was just glad it was summer, which is always an advantage for street life.

28. Lonely

It wasn't just that I felt lonely: I felt betrayed and dumped.

In addition, the language bothered me.

Most of the time I lounged about in the square.

Here, I had no one.

I secretly longed to have back all the stress of Hamburg.

From the few conversations I had with people here, it was clear to me that Germans were not welcome.

Despite the external and internal pressures I stayed in Zurich, and with time I established myself as part of the scenery.

I got used to the people and the language.

I was able to understand them better and I caught myself starting to change how I spoke.

I wanted to belong, because I could not go back.

What's more, I didn't have a passport or any other document, which I could have used for identification.

So I had to be very careful to not attract attention.

I lived on payments from occasional services and the willingness of others to whom I told dramatically sad stories until they softened and gave a few francs.

At night I moved into a basement car park, where I had built myself a not-so-visible sleeping spot.

Here I hoarded everything I owned: a few clothes, candles and an old sleeping bag that I had scavenged from the garbage.

29. The Conflict

Sometimes some strange guys appeared in the square presenting their artistry .

They were fire-eaters, mime-artists, painters and singers.

So it was not surprising when a group of young people with a guitar stood in the square and began to sing Christian songs.

In between a woman told about what she had experienced with Jesus.

A few people stopped.

I was sitting on a bench and watched the bustle from a distance.

It gave some light relief to start making fun of this group.

Some of them appeared slightly uneasy, which increased my delight.

Then a young man rose to speak.

He placed himself on a box to be seen better and read a verse from the Bible, before preaching about it.

He spoke of the love of God.

At first, I thought: "My foot!"

Frustration and disappointment rose up in me.

Why doesn't this God help me, if he exists at all?

Since he apparently knows everything, why does he permit all this misery?

I started to goad myself inwardly, and my anger and rage grew.

I yelled at him and cursed the whole group.

Then I did the unthinkable: I smashed a beer bottle on the edge of the bench on which I was sitting.

With the fragmented bottleneck I went up to the preacher and hit him in the upper body.

I panicked!

Forcefully and quickly I freed myself from the crowd and ran away.

"If they get you now, you are busted. Then the cops will come and lock you up."

Everything in my head was spinning, and I kept on running, until I thought I was safe.

I crept into a house niche in a small alley.

Fully out of breath, I tried to clear my thoughts again.

Now what? Did I have to flee again?

Would I again have to look for another place to live?

I felt overwhelmed at these thoughts, and began to smoke something.

I didn't even have any money: instead I had been living on credit gained through false promises.

The situation was a total mess.

Most of all I wanted to die, so I closed my eyes and waited for doomsday.

30. Who Is Jesus?

When I woke up again, a few hours had passed and I began to feel cold.

I went through cold turkey.

No money, no dope; I felt like death warmed up.

I felt as if my legs were asleep and I couldn't move.

I had to move on, but raising my body was like lifting a bucket of lead.

I began to moan with pain.

Then I heard footsteps and hoped that it was someone I knew.

I lifted my gaze.

"I know that man." My brain tried to work. "I've had it now, he is calling the cops, and I can't get away."

The young preacher was approaching me.

He appeared to be ok, so the injury couldn't have been so serious.

That calmed me down.

Contrary to what I had expected, the man smiled at me and sat down beside me.

"He is stooping down to me, squatting in the dirt and he doesn't mind." I felt embarrassed.

Apart from that, my whole body was shaking and I didn't know where to turn with my life.

He touched me on the shoulder and I winced.

"Can I tell you something about Jesus?" he asked.

I didn't care, I needed dope and so I simply shrugged my shoulders and kept quiet.

Would he tell me anything new?

I had heard everything before and I decided to just let it wash over me.

That was better than being scolded.

The man rummaged in his pocket and brought out a worn-out bible.

He turned the pages as if seeking something specific.

Then he asked for my name.

He described the book as a personal letter to each one of us, one in which we can also insert our own name in the text.

The text, he read to me was from the New Testament.

It was from the 1st Epistle of John, chapter 4, verses 7-10:

"My friends!

Let us love one another, for love comes from God.

Everyone who loves is a child of God and knows God.

Whoever does not love does not know anything of God, because God is love.

God's love for us has become visible to all, as He sent his one and only Son into the world that we might live through him.

The unique thing about this love is:

Not that we loved God, but he has given us his love.

He gave us his son, who took all the blame upon himself, to absolve us of our sins."

Within me I felt a deep longing for something which I could at last define: love and care.

As the preacher read this text, although I was still shivering, nonetheless I listened intently.

What I heard no longer provoked an aggressive reaction from me.

When had I ever before experienced someone relieving me of so much pain?

I felt like a small child in need of help.

He began to talk about this text, about what God has done for us human beings; that he has sacrificed the dearest and most valuable one for our sin and guilt: Jesus Christ, his only son.

What did that mean for me?

Lies, drugs, fraud, unkindness and brutality had filled my life.

Of course, some things which had happened to me could have been blamed on fate.

But was that really the case?

Was I not also responsible for a significant part of it?

Had I not deliberately got involved in many things? Wasn't I also to blame?

Had anyone ever forced me to lie, to take drugs or to sell my body?

Had I not sought that, because I wanted to rebel?

Suddenly I felt quite miserable.

A loser!

There was nothing left in me; my pride and arrogance were gone.

I was helpless and dirty, sitting surrounded by filth, my withdrawal symptoms consuming what was left. I was completely at the end of my tether.

Who could help me? The one who had spoiled everything?

And what was with this God in whom I had never believed?

On the contrary, I had heard a lot about him and I had thought it fun to drag him through the mud.

How often had he been knocking on my heart's door?

Was there still a chance to get to know him in spite of all this?

What could I offer him?

Nothing at all, I had nothing for him; no promises, no good deeds, no goodness as a person.

Only garbage and trash!

I had come to the end of the line and seriously thought I would die.

At that moment the man asked if he could pray with me and if I would give my life to Jesus.

Why would Jesus want to give me a fresh start in life? My life was absolutely worthless.

I was exhausted, broken, and I just thought:

"Why not? It can't harm me anymore. Anyway, I am out of options."

My condition really bothered me; I was sitting there, my hands trembling and my head between my knees.

The preacher began to pray and suggested that I repeat his words sentence by sentence.

I never forgot this prayer, because it was my first personal talk with God.

It was a cry for help in distress.

It completely changed me and turned my life upside down from there on.

The wording was more or less like this:

"Lord Jesus Christ, help me!

Save me.

Rescue me.

Deliver me from the power of drugs and alcohol.

Please, forgive me all my guilt, which I have brought on myself.

Tear up all the chains that bind me and clear away everything that blocks my way to you.

Thank you for dying for me, for going to the cross and paying for my guilt.

I believe that you are the Son of God.

Today, I want to give you my life, completely, with everything that I am.

Come right now.

Take it all.

Transform it.

Amen."

The Bible says that "everyone who calls on the name of the Lord shall be saved."

This is in Romans, chapter 10, verse 13.

Likewise we read in 1John, chapter 1verse 7, the promise that "the blood of Jesus, God's Son, cleanses us from all sin."

After I had spoken this prayer, I felt the coldness disappearing from me.

A warm current ran through my body.

Even more, there was a sense of happiness and security.

It was something I had not known before; something no drugs had given me.

It was something completely new.

A beautiful awareness of life, and I wanted to enjoy it as long as possible.

The man was still sitting with me.

He noticed that I was no longer trembling, and he asked me how I was doing.

I realized at that moment that the effects of the drug withdrawal had completely disappeared.

No yearning, no pain.

I felt good!

But also a great gratitude coursing through, as I realized that I was free of drugs.

No craving returned.

It was a miracle of a supernatural kind, which can only explained by God's love and power.

This is what I want to keep forever.

As I sat in this alley, talking with the preacher, who gave me a small New Testament,

I knew that I needed help to take the first steps of faith.

He invited me to stay overnight in a tearoom run by his community.

Grateful to have a roof over my head for once, I accepted the offer.

The tea room was very cosy, and during the daytime young people met here to talk about faith.

It was a strange feeling, suddenly to be on the other side, walking with Jesus.

But I was happy.

It was an enthusiasm that gripped me.

It was the beginning of my journey with Jesus! I still had a lot of bad habits, as shown one day when I stole the money box from the tea room.

I had always been used to taking what I needed, so I grabbed the box and ran to the next shop.

But then my conscience began stirring and I was not able to spend the money.

I realized that I had done something wrong, so I brought the box back and apologized.

The head of the tea room asked me if I wanted to prepare a short devotion and suggested a short, easy bible text.

I prepared it on a park bench, while smoking a cigarette with a bottle of beer beside me.

Yet when I began reading the Bible, I noticed that what I read there didn't match my outward appearance and behavior.

I stopped smoking and drinking beer in public, because I wanted people to take my newly acquired faith seriously.

So God was working in me and teaching me to go my way with him.

Through this I was also shielded from my fear of the power of drugs.

I had no craving for hard drugs anymore.

I had received a new identity in Christ.

I was convinced that I was wanted and loved by God.

But I also knew that there were still a few important steps ahead of me.

31. My Return

After a period of recovery, I realised that my time in Zurich had come to its end.

The tea room ministry belonged to a Christian movement that had set itself the task of setting up small churches everywhere.

In Switzerland they have their own church network.

But they were also founding churches in Kenya, the Philippines and India.

To further promote this vision they also maintained a bible school.

Here, students were prepared for a missions ministry at home and abroad.

I could imagine just going there for this very purpose, but I wondered if I should complete a vocational training first.

I was very interested in nature and thought about looking for some opportunities in this direction.

However, first I needed to go and ask my foster parents for forgiveness.

This had become clear to me through the many conversations, which I had had with local Christians.

All this time my foster parents had heard nothing from me.

Around this time I realised how painful it must have been for them.

I had done wronged them, and it wasn't easy to go back and face them.

I was thrown back and forth.

In some ways even now I felt rebellious and wanted to blame them for parts of what had happened.

On the other hand I was also aware that I had hurt them deeply.

They had been good to me; the mere fact, that they had accepted me as a matter of course – despite knowing my circumstances.

Although they knew quite a lot about me, they had never revealed to me how much they really knew about my place of birth, my mother and my life in the bar.

Nevertheless they had given me a good home, which I had ultimately treated with contempt.

My heart had softened and I felt remorse and sadness about it.

Since God had forgiven me, I could go and ask for forgiveness myself, where I had hurt and disappointed people.

So I began to plan my return.

It was not easy as many thoughts whirred around in my head.

In fact, it was nothing short of war: at times I was motivated to go and then thoughts of retreating came again.

What is all this?

Why shouldn't I also start a new life?

I was thrown back and forth.

A woman from the tea room supported me with great patience and coaxed me gently to determine that forgiveness and reconciliation were now the order of the day.

No more running away, only going forward.

Understanding this, I started to take action.

I didn't want to fare-dodge any longer or to thumb any more lifts, even though that had become normal for me.

Step by step I had to learn to lead a different, honest way of life.

When I think back to it today, I realise that many people of faith around me very patiently turned a blind eye to my errors!

The staff supported me in my plans and in the end funded a part of the train ride.

So I went back as I had come, without luggage, but I was different.

In my heart I knew that Jesus was with me: I was no longer alone!

On the way I quietly sang songs while intently looking out of the window.

For the first time I perceived the landscape passing by as beautiful.

I took interest in the changing images, the people in my compartment.

Watching a young mother with her two children, the boy maybe 6 years old and the girl still a baby, kept me engrossed for a few kilometres.

The boy sat on my lap, talking about his dad and all that he had experienced during the holidays.

A sense of melancholy arose within me.

A happy child, an intact family, holiday, everything I wanted so eagerly and yet I had never had.

Who was to blame?

Was it fate?

Was it my failure or my mother's?

My foster parents came to mind.

Was it my fault that the relationship had been so poor?

I felt so mean and sneaky.

What had gone wrong?

My train went to Cologne.

Slowly I began to doubt.

Should I really go back?

Having spent all my money, there was nothing else for it but to hitchhike towards the north.

I drank first one beer, then several others, to try to overcome my insecurity.

I ended up in Dusseldorf.

As the weather was good, I would be able to find somewhere to sleep in the city.

The pub streets in the historic town appealed to me.

All my good resolutions and my goal had evaporated away.

I lived in the here and now.

Although I had no money, it was not difficult to get alcohol.

I simply needed an invitation.

I was very good at putting on this show.

Many an acquaintance was slightly irritated by my already advanced alcohol intake.

I stuck with it. The main thing: I was supplied.

Once there were two groups from rival sports clubs at a bar table outside a bar.

I positioned myself and acted as if I was one of them.

One glass followed another and soon I had lost all control of myself.

The beer was followed by brandy and the loose lines.

The consequences were not long in coming.

I became more provocative and aggressive.

I remember being involved in a fight, then I blacked out.

I don't know how long I was unconscious.

It was still evening when I came round, and I was lying in the middle of the pedestrian zone near a large museum.

My head was thumping.

Unsteadily I stood up and held on to the wall.

I stood for a while, simply wanting to see if I could keep my balance. Then I tried to identify my surroundings.

I talked to people and realised that something was wrong.

Something wasn't right with me.

Of course, my alcohol gauge was certainly too high.

I kept trying to recall what had happened.

Something was flickering in front of my eyes and I had a severe headache.

I held my head firmly with both hands, as if I was afraid it might roll off.

Then I began to get my bearings.

Could I remember anything?

It had to be possible to find something that would help.

I felt like an illiterate, not able to link the letters, let alone read.

I desperately tried to remember why I was here in this city.

Not until later did I learn that I had experienced a mental blockage due to a heavy blow.

Here I was again, living on the streets without a goal.

What should I live on; who am I anyway?

Everything was spinning around me.

Then God sent his people, that same evening:

A group of young Christians were having a street outreach, and one of them spoke to me.

He tried to win me round for Jesus and prayed with me.

At that time I wasn't yet sober.

I had drunk a few beers and the sun had been scorching my head the whole day.

It was as if I should once again deliberately turn my life over.

Knowing I had fallen away after my first commitment, I did it.

This time I didn't think so much about whether it would change my life.

It was the result of a conversation about God and his reality in this world but it was different, rather plain, rather than a big emotional experience.

I had a short conversation, received an invitation to a church and then I moved on.

I stayed outdoors although it was still very warm.

The next morning, while it was still quite early and the city still seemed to be sleeping, I washed my hair at a fountain and dried it with my t-shirt.

As it was Sunday, I trotted off looking for the community of the Christians who had had their street outreach the day before.

With my slip in hand, I asked a few passers-by who were already out and about.

I was standing in front of the building way too early.

It wasn't a typical church building.

In the show windows there were religious slogans and references to various events which take place in this building.

I was curious and hours later went there to the service.

What was my identity anyway?

The songs were unknown to me.

Once again, I realized that I couldn't read the slides.

I simply wasn't able to put the words together.

I tried again to remind myself how to learn to read letters and words.

It took time, and a real effort.

Inwardly, I was desperate.

"There is something wrong with me now; I'm crazy - maybe stuck in a trip?"

Some people, who saw my struggles wanted to help me.

I felt like the miracle at the centre of their street outreach.

A family took me home, and I stayed overnight in their living room.

I simply let it all happen.

I felt okay and learned to read the letters amazingly fast for an alleged illiterate.

Gradually, it all came back, but still the question concerning myself remained.

I often sojourned in public places and simply watched the people around me.

During that time, I met a man who pounced on my situation and engaged me in conversation.

He wanted to help me and I permitted that.

I was missing a piece of my own identity.

It didn't bother me that I was diving into a new codependence.

He accepted me like his daughter.

His motives were not completely clear to me.

He told me about his wife and daughter, who had left him some time before, and that he had never coped with that pain.

When he met me, he saw a little bit of his daughter in me and wanted to make amends for what he had missed with her.

I tried to explain my situation to him and how insecure I was.

I knew there was something, but I couldn't see it for myself.

Without any self-control, with nothing in hand, being at his mercy, unable to make my own decisions, the movie went on.

It became a life lesson!

This nice man was a teacher with a social mindset, and he tried to help me.

And then it happened:

Gradually, images and memories came back.

One night I had a dream, and I knew again who I was and where I wanted to go.

It was as if someone was raising the black curtain.

Everything was clear again.

However, what had really happened during the brawl remained untold.

Maybe it was good that I had not immediately returned to my foster parents.

God had his plan!

Otherwise I would never have met these people.

I cann't explain the why and how of this and many other things.

But it was certainly good that I re-dedicated my life and surrendered myself to God.

I realized how unstable I still was, and that the alcohol pulled me under its spell when I was under stress.

I also felt that there are things that I do not have hold of, which I cannot influence.

There was a force and power that took over the throne of my life.

I simply couldn't clarify, change, control or justify anything.

Still today I sometimes find it difficult to explain, to make it comprehensible for people, for them to grasp that there is a higher power that allows and even plans those things, for which we cannot give a logical explanation.

In the Bible there are reports where God does things in people's lives which are inexplicable, but I've learned that you can leave them in God's hands.

One thing remains: God reigns forever in love and truth.

I caught myself being ashamed and thought, what sort of movie is this?

Later, when I became seriously mentally ill, the doctors could still show me that injury from Dusseldorf on the x-ray.

The doctors were amazed that I was so fit.

The medical reason for my failures became evident.

To cope with it I succumbed to fear and helplessness; my pride caused me to be ashamed of myself and to ignore the issue.

In today's ministry, this experience is very helpful to me.

I now know how it feels when something gets lost from memory, and you lose your identity.

Afterwards I felt so stupid that I didn't dare to talk about it and tried to engage in normal everyday life.

However, again and again I have tried to give an explanation for something that is not tangible.

So I thank all those who earlier and later could still accept me with my two personalities and rejoiced with me, that I had come out of this hole.

32. The Prodigal Daughter

I started to plan my trip home for the second time and this time I wanted to reach my destination!

I started hitchhiking north on what felt like an endless journey.

I had to travel the last part by bus.

It was all familiar and yet very strange: this was not my home.

What was I doing here anyway?

I would have loved to turn round at the doorstep, but I had already planned all sorts of things I wanted to say.

First, I sneaked around the house and checked everything out.

I saw how the garden was partially recreated, the garden gate freshly painted and labelled.

Life had continued without me.

Once again I rehearsed my opening lines for when the door opened.

Who was likely to appear first?

I really hoped it would be my father, as I had enjoyed a better relationship with him.

I stood in front of the door for what seemed like an eternity.

Finally, I pressed the doorbell.

To my surprise it was a rather unremarkable reunion.

My mother opened the door and stared at me as if I was from another planet.

We were both speechless.

I couldn't recall any of the words that I had prepared.

None of the emotional outbursts which I had feared materialized.

Eventually, I made my way into the living room, drinking a glass of juice.

Short and sweet, I tried to explain to them what I had done throughout my absence.

I left aside that I had also been involved in prostitution?

I didn't have the courage for this right at that moment.

After I told them about my encounter with Jesus, they were afraid that I was chasing after a substitute for drugs.

They perceived my talking as religious crackpot ideas and asked which sect I was in now and what commitments were associated with it.

For me it was important to ask for forgiveness for everything they had suffered both with and without me.

I realized that I had hurt them so much.

Everything I had learned through the encounter with Jesus, had also changed my attitude towards them.

For me it was important to settle the relationship and to show them that I was very sincere in my apology.

I tried to interact with them in a friendly and accommodating way.

Yes, I really desired that they, too, would come to know Jesusband so it was important to be a witness to them.

They had to see that, indeed, there was a positive change in my life.

God was real to me and that should be noticeable to everyone.

I arranged with my foster parents to be able to stay with them for a transitional period and promised I would do my best to find somewhere else for the longer term.

After such a period of independence it was not easy to adapt to house rules.

This inevitably led to conflicts but with God's help I was able to deal with them differently and was careful to be positive.

Next, it was important for me to seek a Christian community.

I joined a group of young Christians who regularly met to study the Bible and was able to make very good friendships there.

An additional prayer group arose out of it, in which moreover, Martin, my future husband, took part.

In town I started a horticultural apprenticeship and already began to dream of going to a Swiss Bible school.

33. God Is Calling

By this time I had found a congregation for myself, a small city mission with possibly 40 members.

I felt very well cared for in this community and even the size appealed to me; it was like a family.

I attended any event that took place; I went to tent crusades and organized street outreaches.

During the outreaches I was confronted with the Islamic faith because of the high proportion of Turks in town.

I debated and out of curiosity, attended an Islamic cultural centre, that's to say, the areas that were permitted for me as a woman.

I found many things very interesting.

The enforced commitment to community inspired me to go there more often, and the contacts became more intense.

In time I also experienced the pressure that was behind it: the justification by works, without ultimately knowing that you would make it into paradise; the position of women in the Islamic world; instead of grace and love, law and punishment, which govern the believing Muslim.

I read the Koran, surah by surah, and some I even knew by heart.

I discovered a lot of poetry there.

Which religion was the right one?

To be able to lead discussions and argue well and that as a woman, was very difficult, if not impossible.

In spite of that, Islam had cast a spell on me, and I eventually deliberately chose to let go of my copy of the Koran as a symbolic act before eyewitnesses, in order to throw off everything that hindered me from going in the right direction.

I realized the importance of having a sound Christian faith when meeting these people and to share something of the divine truth.

The call to go to bible school became stronger and so I applied to Switzerland.

Back then one month at the bible school cost 300 Swiss francs.

It was money I didn't possess and I explained that to the school principal.

But I knew deep in my heart that I should go there.

I asked the congregation to pray that I would be accepted.

3 months later I got the acceptance for a full-time training in Switzerland.

Linked to it was the anxious desire to make up for my Abitur.

I was glad when I was able to say goodbye to Germany again.

In the bible school there were only 4-bed and 6-bed rooms.

Being in a very small room with five other women was the ultimate challenge for me!

I needed discipline, which I had yet to learn and the whole daily routine was pretty strict; there were hardly any breaks, and punctuality was a basic requirement.

The study time, working time and also the outreaches were so intensively planned that I usually went to bed totally exhausted.

In class there were only 70 students, including 20 short-time Bible students, but by my standards, it was a group size that posed a problem for me.

The house rules were very strict; women and men were separated; there was a dress code, which put me under quite a bit of stress; punctuality and conscientious fulfilment of the duties assigned was mandatory.

Yet, God used even that in order to prepare me for my future ministry.

Without these experiences and learning processes I would never have been able to manage a facility later.

The school encouraged me a lot and I was able to catch up on a lot of things which had fallen by the wayside during school.

I have a sharp brain and learning is easy for me, so many things were simply repetition for me.

During my school years I had also taken my driving license for passenger transportation.

Part of the Bible school programme included a longer outreach abroad.

The class was divided into various teams in order to prepare for the respective country, language and culture.

You could choose from Kenya, India and the Philippines.

I chose Kenya and began to learn songs in the tribal languages of the Masai.

Such a mission trip filled me with a lot of enthusiasm and yet they were weeks that stretched me to my limits in all areas.

There was a field kitchen, where I spent hours peeling potatoes and washing dishes; there were the outreaches in the jungle, which showed me the ease and exuberance of the people despite of all the misery in which they lived, but was hard for me to understand.

And then there was the garage.

The mission society received donations of disused army lorries from Germany.

These were delivered in containers, partially disassembled, and re-bolted together on site.

Help was needed everywhere.

In the meantime I became sick for a time because of the contaminated water.

It was a learning time for me for which I am still grateful.

Everything was guided by God, and I was given only the best training.

Even the story of how I me received the finance was a miracle.

Each student had his own letter box, and I regularly found envelopes with money, which I could use to pay my debts to the school.

God is the provider always, if we trust in him.

He has never let me down, even if sometimes I was placed under huge pressure.

In September of the first year at bible school I was baptised in Lake Constance.

Despite the cold, it was the most beautiful bath ever!

My baptismal verse was Psalm 121, verse 7:

"The Lord shall preserve you from all evil; He shall preserve your soul."

How appropriate for me!

I wrote this Bible verse into my Bible, right at the front.

How many times have I reminded myself of this assurance of God's promise even up to this day.

But the best experience was the infilling of the Holy Spirit.

Once a week we had a prayer night and on one of these evenings the principal came and told us about the revival in Korea and how he had received the baptism of the Holy Spirit.

That was very revolutionary for this pietistic school!

He invited the students, who wanted to have this experience as well, to come forward.

One third of the students responded to this invitation. They received the Holy Spirit and began to speak in other tongues.

At that time it was a difficult thing theologically for such a school.

My faith-believing life moved on to a whole new level.

34. Obedience And Combat

After bible school I went back to Germany.

I tried to attend a German school as I had been advised to do that.

Even though my parents weren't excited about the idea, at least they approved of me gaining a recognised qualification.

I took their indications positively and consented to it for the time being.

The school, which I then chose for myself, turned out to be overly strict and legalistic. It wasn't long before I broke the rules and it was recommended several times that I should leave.

My contact with prayer groups campaigning for political prisoners in Germany motivated me to develop such a circle among the students.

This was met with much scepticism.

There was even fear that I might have a terrorist background, in particular, after I presented paramilitary training groups as types of communities of interest, since they existed in our country and because I didn't condemn them in the strongest terms.

This didn't mean that I sympathised with them and I certainly never intended to indicate that.

I am against sweeping judgements. God sees the individual and his story!

In addition, the school was of the opinion that the practice of spiritual gifts was from the devil and also held other theological views that I could hardly understand.

I knew this was not my place, and I started to cause offense.

I was glad when the school dismissed me, even if I then had no German diploma to boast about.

My foster parents felt it confirmed their belief that such pious people were abnormal and just a temporary trend.

Nevertheless, I followed my Lord and knew deep in my heart, that in everything I experienced and even where I have to take one defeat or another, God was there and had his plan.

I knew that through my life experiences I would have a place working among people on the fringe of society.

It was not quite clear to me how that would take shape, so I looked for a church where I could gain a foothold.

I used the time to absolve a training as a probation officer and enrolled in long-distance university study in the field of social pedagogy while working in a tree nursery in order to make a living.

That was true hard graft.

In any wind and weather I was out, replanting trees, laying out gardens, breaking up flowerbeds.

It was a real muscle-building workout, and through it my immune system stabilized completely.

Apprentices and trainees were assigned to me to guide them in their work.

There were good contacts, and I could tell them a lot about what God had done in my life.

After some time, a young man came with me for Sunday worship services.

My tiny apartment became a gathering place for people from the company who wanted to talk about their concerns and needs.

It was a great time, but I did not stay long, because my church sent me to another city to help a small church to build up their youth ministry.

So once again after almost one year, I moved to the Lower Rhine.

I contacted the tiny Pentecostal church by phone and made my first appointment with them.

When I got there, full of energy, I found only the youth pastor and one young person in the youth meeting.

That was frustrating as I had expected something entirely different.

In fact, there were not virtually no young people at all in this church.

I believe, the youngest couples were in their mid-thirties and still had very young children.

In my eyes it was an aging congregation.

What should I do here?

I felt like dropping the whole thing.

God was the one who kept me there and I heard him speaking very clearly.

Here was my place and here was his youth ministry.

As there were no young people in the church, I had to go out, to where they could be found.

And so I started going with a girl to the streets and the city's parks, where the young people were to be found.

I knew this scene all too well.

I knew what these people would be thinking when we arrived and invited them to join us.

But what I had experienced in my own life, was the best proof that God is real.

His love and power can overcome any barrier, be it external circumstances or our hardened, bound hearts. Jesus has triumphed on the cross and has bruised the serpent's head. And we are, with our lives, the living testimony of this supernatural power stream.

We do not need to do much.

Through the witness of our lives we can easily invite others to know God.

Living authentically is the most important thing!

Whenever we went out into the street, our team grew. We got reinforcements from other congregations, such as a neighbouring congregation, who in turn established a Teen Challenge tea room.

Unfortunately, this church had lost vision for a street ministry of their own, and so they now reinforced our team.

Individuals also came from a Christian children's and youth welfare service and they gave valuable support to the ministry using their professional qualifications and experience.

Then there were also always brethren who prayed a lot, especially at the times when we went to the streets.

Being under God's protection is important in this ministry and every believer can pray.

For that you do not need any special talent or vocation; it is how we communicate with God.

The congregation had an old tea room, where there had formerly been an active street ministry.

The room was a bit musty and outdated, with tiered, stepped seating, covered by an old carpet.

In general the whole thing looked very dark, and structurally as if it had been planned as a garage.

We were desperate for assistance to make something happen here.

I talked to my former youth bible study.

I knew that Martin had started a carpentry training.

I won them and others over, and they helped to demolish the tea room and transformed it into a bright, friendly café.

We had almost no financial resources, so we started to promote it and God gave us donors.

Money was given to cover the cost of wood which was needed, and in addition bistro tables and chairs were also donated. .

It was amazing how God provided for us.

The renovating was also great fun.

Thanks to designing it ourselves and our ongoing work in the parish hall, we drew closer to one another.

This small congregation became a part of me.

I had found a new home and the people who went in and out belonged with me, like a big family.

We felt empathy and joy for one another; friendships grew as we rubbed soulders.

One Sunday I sat in church, and during the worship time I received a word from God.

It was found in Matthew chapter 21, beginning in verse 42 where Jesus said to them (the Pharisees):

"Have you never read in the Scriptures?"

Further Psalm 118 verses 22 onwards continued:

"The stone the builders rejected has become the cornerstone.

The Lord has done this, and it is marvellous in our eyes."

In a parallel passage in Acts 4 verse 11 onwards Peter says:

"That is the stone you builders rejected, which has become the cornerstone.

Salvation is found in no one else, for there is no other name under heaven given to mankind by which we must be saved."

I felt God speaking clearly.

Jesus had been rejected by the builders in a figurative sense, held in low esteem and considered useless.

His value was zero and yet God lifted him up.

He became the mediator between us (sinful man) and God.

Jesus knows what it means to have been pushed to the margins of society.

He knows what the people are suffering who come to our café.

He himself has gone through everything and has paid on the cross for all our guilt.

He feels with you, he suffers with you and is excited about every individual who is saved.

He became the cornerstone, the most important stone in the wall.

This stone would give support to the whole building and also to us, figuratively speaking.

Jesus wants to support us: he is the most important element in the construction of the house wall.

This word would not let me go.

I went forward and shared it with the church, as I wanted them to share in what God had told me.

I related this directly with our ministry on the street and in the café.

We named the café: "Cornerstone Café ".

We had invited the youth groups of the surrounding churches for the official dedication of our café.

They gave us a corner stone engraved with a Scripture.

It received its place at our bar.

But even more important was the presence of our own church who were 100% behind the ministry.

The pastor came and supported us whenever he could, even at the evening events.

On Saturdays he usually went to the pedestrian zone with a stand.

We had some special events with him on the street.

So we invited a tea bus, participated in the Torch Relay for Jesus and were reinforced by Christian musicians.

The youth ministry in church was also involved in the regional youth ministry and we had the opportunity to work here in a fringe group ministry.

People helped us at the street activities that took place in the late afternoons and evenings.

We had so much to do. The café was full. Junkies came and attended our events.

Yet despite these good developments I had to work on myself again and again.

I had already been a Christian for a few years, and yet there were still so many broken areas in my life.

Some accounts of our guests' lives rang a bell with my own experience.

Sometimes I had to be careful not to identify with them too strongly, otherwise I myself would have dived back into my past.

There were also some situations in interpersonal relationships where I had to be careful.

A small conflict right where I was vulnerable could have caused the work in the café to falter.

But despite these lows I went on, and it was nice to see how God generously rewards faithfulness in the little things.

Young families came to church, and the premises became too small.

Martin supported the ministry and always gave me personal support when the going got tough.

The church was behind us as well.

I remember an older brother, who was not able to go with us on the streets regularly, was praying for us during that time and hung cookies and tea on our doorknob.

Through the church I got connected with Teen Challenge (TC).

Teen Challenge is a Christian organization that has taken on the task of helping young people who spend most of their lives on the road and are addicted to drugs.

TC was founded in the USA by the pastor and street preacher David Wilkerson.

What began in the US became established all over the world.

It is a prevention and rehabilitation ministry which is independent of the state and seeks close cooperation with local churches.

I was very interested in it.

A few kilometres outside our town was a former farm, which was the pre- and after-care facility of TC.

The inspiration for this ministry had also originally been through street ministry.

I went to their here converted farm far off in the countryside and had a look.

After some time, I decided to move there and share life in that community.

Living in fellowship with other Christians clearly did me good.

It was another "training camp" where God could train my character and work on my negative traits.

The leader at that time was a good mentor and companion for me.

He knew how to recognise and promote the strengths and talents of others.

I helped outdoors, repaired equipment in the home and was able to participate in cell group ministry and women's ministry.

Once a month there was a women's breakfast with an evangelistic programme.

The farm lived on donations and rental income.

My days were filled up to the brim: street ministry, tearoom, farm, and weekly contact visits with prisoners in a maximum security prison.

I was glad that the number of co-workers had grown.

There was a good team of three congregations with one goal: reaching the lost for Christ.

We went into the highways and by-ways, being present where the need was greatest.

Quite often we picked up one of the prisoners, whom we visited, for a controlled day-parole.

One became a Christian and brought others in the institution in contact with Christians.

Such experiences motivated us, and our ministry expanded.

Very soon there was a Christian contact group in this correctional facility.

Beside this, I wanted to have a job where I could train others.

I knew so many young people who, due to their past, hardly had any chance to get an apprenticeship.

My idea was to build a company, set up with a training workshop.

The only area where I had practical experience, was horticulture.

However, I hadn't worked for a long time and so couldn't show any masters qualification.

So I went to a technical school and became a certified horticultural technician and took examinations to become a trainer.

This had little to do with botany.

It was more like operational management: plant engineering, accounting, technology, human resource management.

At that time I did not realise how important it would be for me in the future.

35. A Life Lived According To God's Calling

With my newly acquired skills I went looking for a job.

I applied to training workshops and factories, and got two lucrative offers.

The first one would have taken me to Florida working for a German company.

I couldn't imagine that, in spite of the good pay.

The second one was a disabled people facility in Bonn, but this was so far away and would necessitate moving.

I could not imagine leaving my church, Teen Challenge and the street ministry.

So I continued with applications, even applying to work for a large youth welfare services provider.

I was invited to a job interview. After making clear to me that they had no open positions in their training workshop, they surprised me with an offer.

Throughout my time in the street and café ministry young people from this institution had visited us again and again. Most of them had run away and tried their luck on the road.

Through our regular opening hours we established a fairly stable relationship with them.

In the eyes of the child care workers they were problem children, with whom they seldom had good access any more.

Now they invited me to work with them and to care for the children as before, but this time with a clear educational assistant's job description.

They were not put off because I was working for Teen Challenge or by my clear Christian orientation and my mission winning people for Jesus.

So, for the first time, I had an employment contract in hand, which clearly stated that I work according to the guidelines of Teen Challenge.

It was a new and unusual situation for me to see my volunteering as a full-time job.

It meant taking on responsibility and I knew I would only be able to make it with God's help as they were not the easiest people to deal with.

Although I myself had a difficult past, I often came to my limits and had to learn afresh how to see these individuals through God's loving eyes.

It was God's plan to call me into this work.

I am thankful that I believed this so strongly as it helped me through, when I was at a loss for how to cope.

One girl, who I cared for within my employment contract, always had the habit of phoning me to confront me with her conflict situations at night after I had gone to bed.

As I was generally dealing with minors, there were certain supervisory duties, so I often got little sleep.

Accompanying young girls to crisis pregnancy counselling centres also belonged to my area of responsibility.

I found it very hard to see some of them wanting to abort unborn babies, even though in their situation it was completely legal.

Even though I did not understand everything, God was my comfort, strength and support in everything.

The cafe was open on three evenings. The rest of the time we went out to the places in the city where the drug addicts and drop-outs met together.

We helped them with minor administrative tasks, brought them, when necessary, to hospital and went with them to court hearings.

Through my work as a probation officer, I wrote reports, statements and assessments for the defendants.

I helped them to find good posts for fulfilling the community service orders imposed on them, and as far as I was able, gave them to the nearby Teen Challenge aftercare farm.

The local Pentecostal church supported us in this.

I was very sure I was in the right place and yet I also knew that I had to take care of myself.

I tended to get caught up in work so that I didn't have enough time for private things.

In this sense the work was also a way of escape from myself.

Even though I knew that I was God's child, my past was often difficult for me.

I am grateful that I had Martin and his parents to support me again and again.

I often went to visit this family and they became my second home. Such a thing was new to me.

This loving way and always open house was a haven for me.

I enjoyed it very much, and so a cordial relationship grew between us.

I had a good friendship with Martin.

36. The Obstacle

It started with terrible migraine-type headaches. I visited several doctors, but my condition worsened.

Sometimes I had such attacks of pain that I went unconscious briefly.

The church members and staff were shocked.

I continued with my ministry on the streets and in the café as best I could, but I often delegated the evening programmes to others.

Martin's father accompanied me for the appointment when my fears were confirmed by a computer tomography: I had a brain tumour just above the right eye.

An immediate operation was ruled out, as it was deemed too risky and instead I received painkillers accompanied by a lot of prayer from church.

Amazingly, I was not as discouraged as some feared.

I knew my life be in God's hands.

God had not done so much for me that I should now be defeated by a brain tumour.

Trusting in this made me strong!

I can still clearly remember taking a long walk around a lake with Martin's father.

We spoke about the promises of God in our lives.

It was the deepest conversation I ever had with him.

There was a noticeable unity, which God granted us at this moment, as we talked about life and death; my life and what God had done in it; my visions and dreams, and how I imagined the next few days, weeks and months.

I had a long intense time of prayer with him.

Finally, we felt certain that God's presence would not leave us, and I had the distinct feeling of being carried.

I deliberately testified about these things, as I felt my circle of acquaintances needed to be cheered up and motivated to believe.

The 1st Epistle of John, chapter 4 came alive for me.

The Bible verses which I had heard at that time in Switzerland, in the house niche, had changed my life completely.

It is the love of God, which carries us and makes us strong.

Verse 16 states:

"And so we know and rely on the love God has for us. God is love. Whoever lives in that love lives in God, and God in him."

This is the essence of God!

It took a few months and then something happened.

I was prayed for at a Teen Challenge conference in Germany.

It was perhaps the fiftieth time, yet I firmly believed that God would grant healing, so I persevered in faith.

The next day I had no more pain!

Once back home, I went to the doctor and another CT was performed.

The tumour was still in the same place, but had encapsulated itself, which meant that the disease had come to a standstill.

Obviously, there was still a regular feeling of pressure, but the extreme pain stayed away.

Hallelujah, praise be to God!

It was an answer to prayer and taught me to trust God in everything.

His will is done, and when we pray in faith, we can await the result in peace.

This applies to all of life's situations and it also applies for the people entrusted to us and those who work with us.

But it is not something we can predict; we must stay dependent on God, which is a good thing.

Unfortunately, it is also true that there is still the reality of God's opponent, who will try anything to separate us from this dependence, to alienate us from God.

Although I often shared my testimony, I also realized that I was holding back more than at the beginning.

And then there was human pride. Our ego, which rules everything, establishes its own rules and limits.

So it was with me.

I was on a road that seemed so clear and straightforward to me, that I forgot that it was God who was actually paving my way.

So I ignored the first small stones, and then I stumbled over the big ones.

In my time at Teen Challenge, I assisted so many people clearing their households before they went to the place assigned to them for therapy.

The dirt, the traces of neglect and drugs were all evident there.

I stood in Duisburg, in the home of an alcoholic, packing the garbage bags with food scraps, packaging, dirty dishes, porn magazines, and used clothes.

It all stank of sweat and dirt.

My thoughts went on a journey.

Very deep inside me something started to move, and I couldn't control it.

A depressive mood arose within me and it became an automatic reaction to grab a bottle of beer to numb the hurt deep inside me.

I was rescued by a hair's breadth from being carried away like an alcoholic.

It was a time when I went through a difficult personal crisis, which was only short-lived thanks to people around me, who watched out for me, lovingly supported me and helped me to find clarity in my walk with God, enabling me to move on without drugs.

In Hebrews, chapter 2, verse 3 it is written:

"How shall we escape punishment if we ignore God's great offer of salvation?"

I now know what happened to me when I neglected prayer; spiritually I ran on empty.

How could I expect that I would escape the consequences of prayerlessness?

I sensed at that moment, how it is when the stream of blessing no longer flows in my life, when the wells of living waters are blocked at the source.

The worries of life captured my time. My serving attitude became replaced with self-pity.

And then came the real warning: my hand began hurting.

At first I thought it was sprained. However, the pain was so intense that one night I went to hospital.

A scintigram was made, but without result.

Then they sent me on spec to the hand surgery department, and it was decided that an operation was necessary.

After the surgery, I felt really bad. I couldn't move.

I learned from the doctor that one of my hand bones had literally been eaten up by a tumour, and they had transplanted a piece of hip bone in my hand.

I had to go for regular check-up appointments.

I was back to square one and it took time until I could function properly again.

Martin visited me regularly and had faith that God would heal me.

My foster parents came to visit, even though they didn't fully grasp the seriousness of my condition.

My encounter with them was rather superficial, but I had a deep encounter with God.

At this moment I again consciously perceived that God was giving me life.

I was dependent on him, and very intentionally so!

From the day when I had given my life to Jesus, I had allowed him to rule my life and to use me: not looking to earthly values, or to human inclinations, but only to Christ for complete fulfilment.

In Colossians 3, verses 1-4 it is written:

"Since, then, you have been raised with Christ to a new life, orientate your whole lives on him.

Look to where Christ is seated on the seat of honour at God's side.

Set your minds on God's invisible world, not on what the earthly world has to offer.

For you are dead for her, but God has already given you eternal life, even if that is now still hidden.

However, when Christ, who is our life, appears, then it will appear in glory that you are living with him."

37. Healing

Whenever I was at the end of my tether, brothers and sisters came to my side.

They came again and again to God for me, with prayer and fasting.

My health condition improved and I bounced back on my feet.

The follow-up appointments revealed that there had been no further spreading of the tumour.

My hand was soon back in normal working order.

I gained new strength and sensed how this healing process had been accelerated.

After one year, apart from the scars, there was no sign of how sick I had been.

Hallelujah!

Alongside this physical regeneration there was also a new spiritual growth.

My attitude changed.

In 1 Corinthians chapter 2, verse 16 it says:

"But we have the mind of Christ."

Jesus had made a decision, when he still was in heaven.

He had made a covenant with the Father to give up his heavenly glory and come to earth as a human being.

He would go down into the world as a servant and he would seek to serve, rather than to be served.

He decided to do the will of the Father and made himself dependent on him.

This knowledge influenced my thoughts.

Is everything that I recognize in myself, a mirror of the nature and mindset of Jesus?

Is my ambition for my own reputation or to serve God?

What is my attitude? Am I authentic as a Christian?

This revelation was more important for me than my physical healing.

Yes, I wanted to serve God, even if it meant making myself a servant to help others.

In Ephesians chapter 4, verses 22-24 we can read what Paul wrote to the church in Ephesus:
"Put off your old self like old clothes.

Do not follow your passions that lead you astray and destroy you.

God's Spirit wants to renew you through and through.

Put on the new life, like you do with your new clothes.

You have become new people, which God has created for himself in his own image.

You belong to God and live as he pleases."

38. An Ambassador Abroad

Even when I was with my friends or in the church, I sometimes felt like a foreigner.

I felt I belonged and could be myself when I was among people living on the street.

When I told others about what God was doing among these people, I felt their sympathy was only surface deep.

Why could no one feel the way I did?

Why were others not inspired so that they would give up everything else to reach these people?

Diaries and calendars were pored over again and again, to find a suitable date for a street event.

Ultimately, the need was still there and only certain days were possible.

I felt driven by this although I knew that my friends found my behaviour quite extreme.

"She's never at home, always on the move."

I could not work up any enthusiasm for sunbathing in the garden or going to a family reunion.

My passion was for the lost people on the streets.

I understood them, I knew their suffering and it was so easy for me to have compassion for them and to stand before God for them.

Again and again I invited them to the café and also to the Sunday service.

So, I witnessed one Sunday how a few of my friends from the city park barged into the service.

Their appearance was in stark contrast to the rather conservatively dressed church members.

In addition they stirred up the service with their heckling and inappropriate contributions, but at the end the pastor made an altar call and a small revival happened.

Street people made a decision for Christ and they shook things up.

They were eager to learn, dragging others to church events. It was simply amazing what God was doing!

At such events, I could sense God was present in this ministry.

It was fun to serve God, and yet at the same time I was declared extreme and a loose horse.

Martin accompanied me when he had time; it was good to be in pairs.

Today I always advise others to minister on the street in pairs.

It is, by the way, a biblical principle: the disciples were sent out in pairs as well.

We had three teams in total, which were on the street regularly.

Mostly they came back with café-guests.

Good relationships developed and many people grew very close to our hearts, but there were also defeats.

We had to be as cunning as foxes to ensure that our café did not become a drug trans-shipment point.

The toilets, as well as the dark passageway between the café and the church hall, were all critical zones.

We did not want to fall into disrepute with this good work.

On occasion we had to warn our friends and even to throw them out.

Many a night ended with a ride to hospital with a young man who was going through a withdrawal with us or suffering from an acute poisoning.

And yet our message stuck positively with most of them: we take care of you and the love and power of Jesus can also reach and liberate you.

39. Wedding

Martin and I had been together now for quite a while.

I had come to love and appreciate his family.

Yet one question remained in the room. Was our vocation a shared one? Should we both be in the same ministry? Were our personalities cemented together by love? That did not sound romantic!

It had nothing to do with a lack of mutual affection and love, which were also present!

Rather than being just blindly in love, we were standing together in a living, personal relationship with our God.

So it was that we had lively discussions about our visions and ideas, and concluded that we both felt the same vocation for fringe group ministry; Martin, through experiences in his family, tended towards mentally disabled people, while I, due to my background, veered towards vulnerable, independent people.

As I was already working for Teen Challenge, we had a couple of weeks of holiday and travelled to the various facilities of Teen Challenge in Germany.

We received feedback from co-workers and leaders, let people pray for our journey, took part in outreaches and experienced again and again, how totally broken people were released from their constraints and addictions.

There were no complicated application procedures for admission to therapy, yet those who asked, received help and were accompanied in prayer.

I remembered a passage from the book "The Cross and the Switchblade" by David Wilkerson, founder of Teen Challenge, where the following scene was described:

David was preaching on the street in front of representatives of the youth gangs.

In doing so he met Nicky Cruz.

He said to David, "If you come closer to me, I'll kill you!"

David replied, "You could cut me into one thousand pieces and spread them on the road, and each piece would love you."

God's love was in the foreground: this was what the people on the street should experience.

That was what brought blessing for the individual.

During this time we realized that we shared a common "Yes" to David Wilkerson's basic spiritual philosophy.

So we did an internship in a treatment centre for women from drug backgrounds.

Martin helped by giving instruction and I was more involved in administrative processes.

We got to know the principles and objectives of inpatient facilities at Teen Challenge and loved it.

I was somewhat captivated by the thought that it would have done me good to come to terms with my injuries and shortcomings in such a protective setting.

Here love was pure; you could even touch it.

A feeling of melancholy welled up in me, but I suppressed it again.

Martin was happy here as well.

He loved to work with the wood machinery and produced a new lectern for our services.

During summer 1989 we became engaged in the small basement chapel of this institution, something which did not remain hidden from the leadership.

In the middle of the night it was the only room that was lit up brightly.

It was also a symbolic act for us to begin our married life at Teen Challenge.

We had found a home together in one ministry.

A ministry whose vision was to reach the lost, the broken, the people, whom most others ignored, and show them a way out of hopelessness.

One year later we got married and moved into the apartment above our café.

Martin worked as a carpenter 13 km outside the city.

I continued my social work as an educational co-worker at a youth services facility and was also a director of the Teen Challenge café ministry.

A young lady, named Marion, who was trained as a child care worker, supported our ministry and soon became an indispensable part of the café.

She had good contact with our guests.

Marion was a valuable employee and her sense of humour helped us through some difficult situations.

She had a creative streak which brought new ideas to the café and was good for our visitors. Very soon she filled in for us when we could not be on the street outreaches.

Her special way of caring for the addicts in the park, meant taking them seriously, and yet knowing where their personal limits were.

No one was permitted to lose their cutting edge.

She was gifted in respecting each one's unique personality.

In time we had several street teams.

Whenever one or two teams were on the street, they were supported by others in thought and prayer.

They were always in pairs and often they came back with people in tow.

It was very encouraging to see how our offer was perceived by the people on the street.

Marion moved to the Teen Challenge farm in Kerken.

There she found the Christian community, of which she had dreamed.

It was a very good time for her.

Often we shared with one another and rediscovered once again how valuable it can be, to live committed to people in such a deep way.

In October 1990, Martin and I made a special trip to Berlin for a week.

It was something of a belated honeymoon.

Again we visited the Teen Challenge ministry: the Tearoom on Kurfürstenstrasse and also the centre in the Rütlistrasse.

This was where Teen Challenge had begun in Germany.

When the ministry first came to Europe, it had started in Amsterdam.

The second city back then was Berlin.

It was very moving, as we sat at the table with the then-leaders, and they told us how they had found their way to Teen Challenge.

This encouraged us in what we were doing and we were glad to be there.

This package of street ministry, therapy and aftercare, all from one facility, made the ministry very effective.

We were at the beginning, on the frontline, where we could meet people in their distress and were able to show them a way out.

I was grateful at this point to be together with Martin.

During this time we received the news that Marion had suffered a fatal heart attack at her work.

It was difficult for us to understand the loss of a much cherished person.

At the funeral, I felt for the first time that I was able to express my grief through tears.

In retrospect, I am very, very grateful for that!

How precious it is to be able to cry at times.

40. Finding Our Way As A Couple

We felt very comfortable in our apartment in the parish hall.

Our bedroom, which was part of the church hall annex, faced out into the garden.

A few times, after a busy café night we allowed ourselves, with the windows open, to eavesdrop on the Sunday sermon while lying in bed. Actually, the apartment was a bit too spacious, being 100 square meters in area.

Because of this, we had many opportunities to invite people around and even to let one or the other stay overnight, after an evening in the café.

For us as a young married couple, it was not so easy to still have enough time for ourselves besides the job, the church, Teen Challenge, the family and friends.

We almost had to establish a timetable to define our private hours.

Usually the calendar defined the week: everything was well organized, and yet we still tried to be flexible when people came to us in desperate need.

The shared times of prayer and the study of God's Word remained important and valuable to us.

Sometimes we connected as we prepared a devotion, or as we referred to the previous Sunday's sermon.

Since we were living in the parish hall, we were also confronted with some caretaking services.

And so we also had to deal with the situation when church members spontaneously "borrowed" the keys while I was mowing the community garden lawn, or when others, who wanted to clean the stairwell, demanded that we should make time for a chat over a cup of coffee whenever it suited them.

Sometimes it was amusing, but often it was just plain exhausting.

Today I look back on it all as a time of training.

Without this learning environment, neither of us would have taken the step of leading a therapeutic facility.

God confirmed again and again that we were on the right track, and we got support from the Landesjugendwerk (BFP).

Youth groups visited us, and we had street outreaches together.

Christians from other communities and churches showed an interest and ministered with us.

In Duisburg, there was already the TC Tea Room "Oasis", with whom we had close contact and a youth bible study group from the Evangelical Church.

It was a great encouragement, in particular on this interdenominational path, to just point out that Christians can draw people to Jesus as they stand together in unity.

I realised afresh that the most important aspect of the Teen Challenge ministry isn't the buildings or finances; it is the staff, who fully dedicate themselves to the vision, to faith and mercy, reaching out to the lost for Christ.

Evangelism is the fundamental element.

We can't wait until the fish come to us on their own and swim into the net.

No, we need to cast the net where the fish are!

By his calm, composed manner, Martin even understood how to bring together a diverse team with all their different ideas, and this ultimately brought about greater effectiveness.

Whereas I was rather visionary, he had the gift of sorting everything into organized structures and sometimes brought me down to earth, for which I am, in retrospect, grateful even today.

41. Street Kids

Whereas in the beginning people from the city's fringe scene used to visit our café, we realised over time that our clientele had changed.

Younger people, i.e., teenagers, were coming to us, seeking friendship and assistance.

Often the cause of their difficulties were problems at school, family crises or neglect.

As usual, some of them were also referred by the child and youth services.

What should we do?

What we offered was designed for much older visitors.

We shifted our opening times to the afternoon and evening, but we realized that these young people needed more than a couple of hours of care.

They needed a stable home, a daily routine, school guidance etc. We prayed with the staff.

What should we do?

Was this pour calling?

Did God send us these people to bring transformation?

Sometimes it's important just to move forward and see where God leads.

So I went to my desk and started to draw a concept for a rural property with animals as they are a great educational tool.

I visualised a vast landscape, a good church nearby and plenty of living space, a workshop and much more.

The ideas tumbled out of me just like that.

In between I shared my thoughts with Martin over and over again.

How old or young should our clients be, should we admit girls or boys or both?

How should the day be organized?

What about school and training?

One question lingered, which was typical for me:

Who would pay?

Since I was Christian I had never lacked anything.

Somehow it was also clear that it was essential for us to be affiliated to a church.

It took weeks until the concept of a farm, where we wanted receive teens, was ready.

I submitted the whole project to our supporting regional council for approval.

Then there was a long period of waiting.

It took weeks, and they seemed to us like an eternity.

Shortly before our first planned vacation since our wedding, we received their response, which really inspired us.

The Regional Council had approved the draft, conditional upon us employing people with professional qualifications, and gave us an operating license to run as an independent educational establishment.

Of course, by nature I would have preferred to start the search for a suitable farm as soon as possible, but it was good that our schedule provided for vacation first.

We needed this recovery bolster.

42. The Farm

We returned from Austria feeling relaxed, although I had I hardly stopped talking about the new project, and started searching for the right property.

We decided to search a rural area within a radius of 30 kilometres for a former farm or similar.

But without success!

We found two alternatives: either the building was unaffordable, because all the buildings with a solid infrastructure had already been snapped up by other house-hunters, or it was a ruined building and would have required us to invest a fortune to do the repairs to make it fit for habitation.

Although we were on the lookout for a long time, the doors seemed to be tightly closed.

Again and again we brought the issue before God. In response we received a Bible text from the prophet Isaiah.

It is found in Isaiah chapter 61, verses 1-3:

"The Spirit of the Lord is on me, because he has called me.

He has sent me to preach good news to the poor and to comfort the ones in despair.

I proclaim freedom for the captives, their bondages are now released and the prison doors are opened.

I say to them:

"Now, God redeems you from your guilt". But now the time has also come, that the Lord gets even with his enemies.

He has sent me to comfort all who mourn.

The time of suffering of the inhabitants of Jerusalem is gone!

They do not, full of despair, scatter ashes on the head, but adorn themselves with a turban.

Instead of mourning robes I give them fragrant oil which they will delight.

I want to turn their discouragement into joy, which will adorn them like a festive dress.

Who then sees them, will compare them with trees planted by the Lord.

They will be called "Garden of the Lord", in which he shows his greatness and power."

It is a text which points to God's love and power, awakens hope and indicates a clear approach. It was the Launchpad for the ministry, to which we have been called by God.

This didn't help us in finding a suitable farm, but it confirmed that we were on the right path.

Through this, God was calling us into ministry.

We had been praying for a long time and wondered why it had taken so long, why nothing visible had happened.

Here was a moment when God was clearly speaking to us and teaching us.

Martin and I heard it independently:

"Let go, go where ever I will lead you, do not mourn old bondages, leave your families, your congregation and friends, and follow me." That sounds easy from the outside, but it is not!

We went to Martin's parents, talked to our church, and obtained their blessing for this step.

Lo and behold, the incredible happened: God began to open doors!

By choosing to have a larger search radius, the real estate market had more to offer.

So we took a look at farms in the Westerwald, the Hunsrück and also in northern Germany.

Most of them had not been inhabited for a long time.

We read the advertisement we were looking for in a Sunday paper.

They were advertising a disused farm in Emsland.

Martin had no time to go there, so I drove down with a friend, who had more knowledge about houses than I did.

After 100 kilometres, the motorway ended and we had to drive twice as long on the ordinary road.

It seemed to me, as if we were on the go for ever.

The farm was outside a small town, nestled in the countryside and about 400 metres away from the Dutch border.

The farm owners were very nice and showed us everything.

They were older and were looking forward to move to the next village, to reach shops and doctors more conveniently.

Their children didn't want the farm.

In the next village, there were a restaurant, savings banks and two small shops where you could buy the basics.

Two kilometres away, on the same street as the farm, was a carpenters'.

I wrote down the phone number and address.

In many respects I liked the farm and the surrounding area very much.

It had something which I couldn't describe, but I simply felt good about it.

The owners wanted to sell as soon as possible.

My mind was full of impressions as I told Martin about it in the evening.

In addition to the many positive things I had to say, I gave Martin the address of that carpentry.

Martin contacted the carpenters' and we decided to go there for a second visit.

The boss was still looking for a worker and Martin applied there.

We also took Martin's parents with us on our visit to Emsland.

For us it was important to share our thoughts with them and to pray for the right decision.

Once again, I was overcome by a feeling of peace and could well imagine living here.

But nothing was certain yet.

We needed the money for the purchase of the farm and Martin needed a job that was accessible by bike.

We also wanted a clear acknowledgement from God and it was important to us, to have a church nearby.

We remembered that already before our wedding, Martin and I had often received a parish newsletter from a Pentecostal congregation in Leer.

At that time I had asked this church to not send us anything, since we had no relation to Leer.

As we now looked at our road map, Leer did not seem to us so far away from Hasselbrock village.

So I called the pastor and told him about ourselves and the plans to eventually move to the Emsland.

I made an appointment to get to know the church.

It was not the usual church service which we experienced there, since it was celebrated in a school hall and yet we received a good impression.

The worship was lively, the church was well represented with all generations and the sermon was easy to relate to.

We felt comfortable, and of course the first impression is usually very important.

Afterwards, the pastor gave time to us as we explained to him the importance of having a church behind our ministry, sustaining us in prayer and providing us with a spiritual home.

Pastor Hartmut Knorr took our concern to the church board and promised us feedback soon.

How this came about through the church newsletter was really strange, but it helped us to find a church nearby.

By that I mean, it was still 45 kilometres away from Hasselbrock.

This was okay, considering the rural nature of that area and that northern Emsland is consistently Catholic, with hardly any free churches, in which we could plant our spiritual roots.

Thanks to the good motorway connection, Leer could be reached quickly.

Now, everything else needed to work out.

In our church we talked enthusiastically about the opportunity of possibly acquiring a farm in Emsland.

Even if the place was now further away than we had wished, enthusiasm grew and was passed on to others.

We gave the management of the café ministry into other hands.

We knew that with the new leaders a restructuring of the ministry would take place, but that it would remain a fringe group ministry.

Today, there is a Christian counselling centre under the umbrella of Teen Challenge named "Totally Normal."

It is an important learning step to hand over tasks again at the right time, and to trust God that He holds everything in his hand.

None of us is irreplaceable!

One day Martin got a reply from the joinery in Hasselbrock to say that they wanted to hire him immediately.

This was the first confirmation for us that it could work out with the farm.

We were overjoyed when we then received incredible news of an interest-free loan to help with half of the purchase of the property!

We checked with the banks and found a financial institution that would give us acceptable terms for the second half of the payment.

In June 1991 we bought the farm and called it: Hasselbrock Project Farm (Projekthof Hasselbrock).

Our vendors had bought a house, but there was some trouble and they still continued to live on the farm until the end of November.

As a birthday gift we received five chickens from friends as a seed money for the farm; keeping them was quite an adventure for the first two weeks.

On 1 December 1991, we moved in along with our hens.

Now Emsland was our new home.

Our reception was cold and foggy.

The kitchen was heated with an old stove which burned peat briquettes.

Besides our personal effects we also brought a lot of donated furniture.

So we moved into the former dwelling house and renovated it room by room.

Everything was very simple.

We had chosen the largest bedroom to be our private quarters.

Here, we also accommodated our office.

On the ground floor was the kitchen, the dining room, the living room and our room.

On the first floor there were three bedrooms and a bathroom.

A fourth room was in the attic, and it became the focus of our first reconstruction work: it was converted into another bedroom.

In early 1992 two young people, whom we had already cared for in the Lower Rhine, came to us.

We regularly attended the Free Evangelical Church (Freie Christusgemeinde) in Leer and became members.

Apart from that, our days were filled with caring for adolescents, giving school support and building repairs.

Martin worked at the carpenters' and I gained a contract with my former employer, to accept young people he recommended to us.

This enabled us to manage well financially, and we paid off the loan as quickly as possible, so that we could focus on the necessary house renovations.

The farm was incorporated into the confederation of Teen Challenge Germany.

Our work was recognised by the youth welfare authorities, and we were described as running a mini group home for children and adolescents.

In the beginning one girl and one boy lived with us.

After the girl left our facility, we decided to only accept boys.

In the beginning we offered two intensive care places and then expanded to three places.

When one of the youths slipped into a phase where he found it difficult to regain his independence from the farm, we began to look for an outside unit.

Much wisdom, creativity and imagination was needed!

So, just like Peter Lustig from the popular TV show "Dandelion" (Löwenzahn), we got hold of a construction trailer for expansion. On the outside we renovated the roof, inside it needed a wooden panel and was provided with electricity, heating and water.

The teenager moved cosy furniture into it and thus created his new home.

In addition, we found a mariner who took our adolescents onto a ship, we bought a cost-effective caravan and a boy was offered an internship on a horse ranch.

We undertook outreaches and escorted relief transport to Romania, where we had street crusades and intentionally distributed food and clothing.

A teenager who had come with us, also played guitar and spoke quite candidly about his life and his relationship with God.

Something like this was always very encouraging.

This tour to Romania opened my heart wide for this country.

In love with this country and the people who live there, I could have wanted to stay there much longer, had time permitted.

Martin felt similarly and we dreamt of going back to this country one day.

However, we also experienced very unpleasant things on this tour.

In Brashov we had a traffic accident, in which a police car crashed into us.

If it had been done intentionally or not was never clarified.

We were able to bring the car to a garage and the car breakdown company took over.

It quickly became apparent that it needed to be brought to Germany to ensure that everything would be repaired correctly.

Now we didn't have a car any more, and our outreaches were limited.

One Bible school, where we were staying, had an "object of faith" on four wheels.

We used this car for short trips.

It was a real adventure!

But throughout all our calamities, it was the helpfulness and care shown to us by these people, their generosity and commitment, which really made an impression on me.

Of course there were cultural and even linguistic barriers, but it did not stop us loving these people and wanting to understand them.

Perhaps we will head back to this country one day, who knows ...

We continued in Hasselbrock, knowing it was our place.

It was a ministry under construction, which had enormous struggles finding its place in the village.

How should I get it across to them that we offered more than just a social service for "difficult people"?

What motivated us was our common vocation: in serving, giving people hope, showing them a way out of their situation and exemplifying this by our lives.

And all of this without looking at what benefits it might bring us!

I could only smile when people asked such questions: it was a 24/7 ministry, which demanded everything of us and where we lived very closely with one another.

Our privacy was limited to one small room.

Again and again we looked for new opportunities, starting from where these young people were and engaging them in meaningful projects.

We started to support the Royal Rangers ministry alongside the congregation in Leer.

We offered the Scout divisions space for camps and tried to integrate our young people there as well.

I even took part in all sorts of Royal Rangers training camps and was an instructor in some camps to train staff.

We had cycling tours with our young people down to Sauerland and organized outings and experiential learning activities.

The children and young people who came to us were aged 12 to 16 and could be in our care until they turned twenty-one.

We integrated them in the church events, as best we could, and some of them settled in our area after the official care period ended.

We didn't find it easy to lead young people to Christ.

Often I was reminded of how crabby I was way back then.

There was so much rebellion and hurt. Again and again we received support from employees who we hired for certain tasks.

In doing so, we were very mindful that they needed to share Teen Challenge's vision.

In addition to the ministry on the farm we placed people into Christian therapy facilities.

For several years we had been a member of the ACL (Arbeitsgemeinschaft Christlicher Lebenshilfen) – Christian Social Support Association. We attended conferences, and were encouraged by the exchanges and expertise.

We saw that others had similar problems and conflicts, but that with God's help there is always progress.

God led us, shaped the ministry and provided us with everything that was needed.

Through the ACL we came to know various nation-wide Christian support ministries.

We had long been the only facility that could accommodate children and adolescents.

However, we noticed over the years that this obliged us to make certain commitments to the authorities.

The child welfare support, for which we were working, was in continuous negotiations with the State Youth Welfare Office in charge of Lower Saxony regarding the recognition of micro-homes.

In addition to the ACL meetings there were regular meetings of the Teen Challenge ministry.

Many structural changes took place in the individual facilities during our years as members.

More and more "guests" started to take the therapy places at the request of our sponsors.

The placement of a drug addict had become a complex procedure.

Reception houses, like Berlin, were trying to bridge the time well and to keep their people motivated, but something had got lost in the whole thing.

It was at this time that the thought of returning to our roots came.

Yes, where were they, the roots?

At first I personally struggled a lot with this idea.

I went to the leadership meetings, really wanting to look forward rather than back.

However, the next Teen Challenge seminars were under the slogan: "Back to the roots", which was raised a personal question to everyone:

How did it start?

What had it been that called and drove us into this ministry?

What had we experienced with God's help?

In response we recalled the testimonies of people on the street who were liberated from their addictions and obsessions, people who gave their old lives to God and dared a fresh start.

How many times had the word of God come alive through Isaiah 61, where it is written that God gives freedom?

God was the same then, as he is today!

He is the one who wants to work through us now as he did a few years ago.

It was a challenge of faith: do I believe that God works, supplies, delivers?

Can he use me when I continually put my trust in him, and do I trust him more than the social system of our country?

Paul writes at the beginning of Romans:

"I am not ashamed of the saving news.

It is the power of God.

It liberates everyone who trusts in it: first the Jew, then everyone else.

For in it God shows how He is:

He ensures that our guilt is atoned for and we can have fellowship with Him.

This happens when we rely only on what God has done for us.

So it's already in the Scriptures:

"Only he will find God's approval and live who trusts Him." (Romans 1, verses 16 and 17)

Martin and I were in the process of going back to our roots, even if we did not yet understand that ourselves.

A milestone in this process was also a change of church.

As a rule, I think we should commit to a local congregation and I do not advise people to cruise around the church world!

But with us there was a development: due to a change of pastor and the ensuing shift in focus, the fringe group ministry became an orphan.

It was difficult to maintain the contact since, in addition to the emotional distance which we felt, geographically we were also 45 km apart.

Having lost the spiritual support which had once formed the basis of our relationship with the congregation, we were looking for a new home.

So we ended up at Christ Church, Weener. (Christuskirche Weener)

New contacts with fresh spiritual insights breathed life into the ministry on the farm.

More and more our process of going "Back to the Roots" was spiritually inspired. This congregation had a strong missionary orientation, from which new congregations sprang up in our vicinity.

So we decided to actively support a church plant.

43. Teen Challenge - Back To The Roots

For nearly ten years now we had received children and adolescents onto our farm.

Thanks to our contractual obligations to the child welfare body in North Rhine-Westphalia, we were well taken care of financially.

Meanwhile, Martin passed his master craftsman examination and opted to be a co-worker on the farm.

Our young people were cared for with a staffing ratio of 1 worker for 2 young people.

Over the years many things were renovated and the facilities expanded.

Then came a change in the jurisdiction of the region's Youth Services and our facility was put to the test.

The home supervision authorities visited, along with the fire prevention officials, the sanitation officials etc. Although we complied with all our obligations, we experienced it as a kind of harassment.

The crowning glory was the questioning of our professional qualifications.

So it was no longer enough to be a social educationalist to manage the facility, no, you needed to be trained as a practical educator.

We could not provide proof of this.

So Martin and I decided to go to school again, to meet the minimum requirements: to become trained social assistants.

That was not so easy, because the work and care had to keep running on the farm and we already had two small children at this time.

A young woman from our church came to work with us, taking care of our children and relieving us as a family of many pressures.

We were very grateful for that.

At school, it was a pretty unusual picture.

The teachers couldn't quite work us out, as we had already spent quite a few years working and handled the workload of qualified professionals.

During this time we were expecting our third child.

Anna Lea was born even before the final exam.

Although, on the one hand, school was cumbersome and added to our workload and time pressures, still we benefitted from the the interaction with the teachers.

Yes, they was good times to talk shop about youth services and at the same time,.to look at the bigger picture

We gained contacts with other similar organizations.

We also took advantage of this opportunity by sharing our vision and Christian foundation.

At Christmas time, we invited the entire class to our farm and performed a joint nativity play.

Once we had passed our exams and finally met all the criteria for approval of the home, we realized that change was in the air.

My employer wanted to change the contract, in ways that wouldn't have benefitted us, which led to many conversations, but we were not able to find a win-win situation.

Apparently the child and youth welfare services, did not want to support our Christian orientation.

It was just difficult and got on our nerves.

Suddenly, I was sure that there would be a change on the farm.

Martin and I prayed a lot about how we should move forward.

And there it was again, the challenge concerning our original motivation: where were our roots?

We wanted to live in God's calling and not gratify any authorities.

Whenever we are wrapped up in our daily work routines, day in, day out, it is important to pause every now and again and go back to where it began.

- We can drive a car for a long way without refuelling; sometimes using more throttle, sometimes less; being on the road in urban areas, car parks or on an open range.

I could equate these driving experiences in my daily life with our lives and calling.

The open range represented the crusades, the missions; the guest services ...

The narrow alleys which we had to drive through in the cities, represented the many instances when we were squeezed for time, trying to juggle church, work and quality family life.

It took careful planning to ensure that one commitment wasn't in competition with another.

The parking areas symbolised the freedom of free weekends and holidays.

But eventually our car began to splutter.

The fuel gauge told us: Refill, otherwise you won't be able to go anywhere!

We do need gas stations in our lives.

There is no way around it: it is a necessity.

However, it is advisable to fill the tank before setting out on a long haul and not to just hope there will be opportunities to retank when we need to, or living in fear that we may run empty.

Maybe we think we have enough, but find ourselves in a traffic jam or find that the price has doubled, and we may even start to get angry with ourselves:

"If I had ..."

I want to encourage you to first go to the gas station, to fill up on the energy to go forward, to run, to drive.

Throughout my life I often experienced such a personal "energy crisis". Again and again I thought:

"I'm doing fine, I will make it ..." Here an appointment, there a conversation, at the same time caring for the children, and then suddenly comes the point where you are wiped out.

I am at a dead end, the family suffers and nothing I do, helps.

It was difficult for me to admit that I had failed to fill up with energy at the beginning, when I needed to.

Internally, I was wrestling with myself.

But Bettina cannot succeed when she is strong!

It took time until I got to the point where I acknowledged I needed help.

Excusing myself from everyday life events, I started to allow myself time off, time to do nothing.

Resting, walking, having regular conversations with God and also allowing the team to carry me.

"I was off!" That was totally okay for the community on the farm. In the course of time, I realized that new strength grows out of "idleness", God gave me His peace.

I was refilling my tank and, what was also crucial, I was already looking for the next gas stations, where I would be able to rest and receive fresh power.

I had to give myself permission to be weak and tired once in a while. Since then it has become easier for me to pay attention to the display readings on my internal-reserve tanks before any crisis looms.

We each have our own type of engine but the energy source remains the same!

Maybe I need regular petrol to proceed, while others need 'super'.

But a full selection is available at the gas station, and it is the same with spiritual energy.

For ministry, we need fuel.

Isaiah chapter 61, verses 1-4 are the strapline for the farm:

He anoints me, he fills me up, provides the energy for me, which I need to travel along my route.

Then I can start on my journey.

I must fill up on the right resources for my needs.

And now it is vital to pay attention, to set my navigation system, to make sure that I will get to my God-planned destination.

Out of these experiences, the following thoughts became important to me:

There are obstacles in our spiritual lives that can be compared with road traffic.

Roadworks diversions show us we can't follow our usual route. We must go a round-about way.

Traffic jams teach us patience, perseverance and give us the opportunity to reset our priorities, goals and perspectives. In our usual mobile, fast-moving world, they warn us not to lose focus!

Staying with the car illustration, we all know that many a person experiences a breakdown in some way or other: and I am not excluded!

Decisions that do not match the situation and timing, and doing a U-turn with decisions already taken are difficult, and cost hard-pressed explanations, but they are lessons we have to learn.

If we do not learn them, we may find that our car isn't roadworthy.

Often we lose our way and it takes time to get back up to speed.

En route to my destination, I can vary how fast I drive.

Sometimes there are guidelines from the outside, which I should follow.

God always adds a timetable to our mandate, and we must take account of policies, limits and schedules.

We should definitely make the effort to study them thoroughly, because the worst thing that can happen is to have an accident or even worse: to cause it!

We don't always assess a situation properly and may even face life-threatening consequences.

Maybe we run into a brick wall, and find ourselves in a stalemate situation, where the most important thing is to acknowledge our need for help and healing.

My mandate will have to be suspended or be changed.

I may find myself taken off course for the time being, but, and this is very important, even then I am not released from God's plan and purpose.

I think of how many breakdowns, accidents and diversions those chaotic disciples of the Bible experienced, and still Jesus held them.

The apostles were chosen from among them, including Peter, who had hit a brick wall, wanting to follow Jesus at all costs, but then having denied him.

The first Epistle of Petergraphically describes the status and purpose given to us by God Himself. In chapter 2, verse 9 it says:

"You are a chosen people, a royal priesthood, a holy nation, a people belonging to God, that you may declare the praises of him who called you out of darkness into his wonderful light." Knowing and understanding this is like holding the driver's license for a car or the ticket for a train in our hand. Imagine what can happen when we live by faith in confidence of all that God can do through us.

In Isaiah 61 it is explained and broken down into details:

I have been anointed:

• To preach good news to the wretched
• To bind up the broken-hearted
• To proclaim freedom for the captives
• To announce the opening of prison doors for the prisoners
• To preach a year of grace of the Lord and at the same time a day of vengeance
• To comfort all who mourn
• To provide for those who grieve in Zion and bestow on them a crown of beauty instead of ashes, the oil of gladness instead of mourning, a garment of praise instead of a spirit of despair.

And they will be called:

- Oaks of righteousness
- A planting of the Lord

For the display of His splendour!

And then something wonderful happens: they will rebuild the ruins and restore the places long devastated, they will renew the ruined cities that have been devastated for generations.

That means, the deceased will alive again!

This is the driver's license and travel card which we are holding.

These are the promises and statements of God for the farm.

That's the calling, into which God called us many years ago.

He gave us the competence because he has faith in us.

He gives us everything necessary to complete his mission.

Here is the source of our energy, and we must not forget to periodically refuel using the correct type of fuel.

What happens if I fill up my diesel car with regular petrol?

In the long run, the car will be unable to drive.

In my spiritual life, it is also very important for me to draw my supplies from the right energy source.

If I run after the media to get replenished there, instead of seeking the presence of God, or follow the numerous possibilities of meditation and mind expansion which have absolutely no Christian reference at all, I'll find that in the long run I will run out of strength to minister for the kingdom of God. We have a ticket to a specific goal.

We are dealing with people, who are living on the margins of society.

They matter to God; so he calls us to help these people and sets us free to do so.

We are to care, build and strengthen, and then release them into independence from us.

We should not lose out of our focus:

These people will be rebuilding the old debris, renewing cities, revolutionizing what laid fallow for generations.

Social ties, behaviour patterns, bondages, diseases; ... they will reset them, because they have come from death to eternal life.

They will be healed in body, soul and spirit.

We are not to lose our focus, but should anticipate seeing this, we should long for it, as we follow our calling.

This confirmed to us that we had not merely been busy with a construction site or arrived at a dead end.

We had received the calling for ministry 10 years ago, and in spite of occasional diversions, we recognised that God has fully qualified us as we read in the Bible:

"Thus, by their fruit you will recognise them."

(Matthew chapter 7, verse 20)

At this point, I am grateful for this visible fruit: obvious changes that prove what is happening on inside of the individual.

For many years I have been writing down stories, thoughts and changes I have seen.

It is wonderful to see how God's existence and power are always available.

It is my wish that this launchpad, Isaiah chapter 61, verses 1-4 will deeply challenge more people to be engaged in this ministry.

These few Bible verses could fill many sermons, but the first verse is and remains for me the key, to the success of our mission:

"The spirit of the Lord is upon me, because the Lord has anointed me ..."

That's my fuel, my source of energy!

God inspired us anew and we began to walk in faith.

There was still a vacant pigsty, with space for 250 pigs for fattening, on the farm.

So far, it had only served as a storage space.

We were under the impression that we should redeem the time, as long as we still had regular income.

So we began to convert the pigsty into a modern joinery.

Martin was a master and our idea was to build a financial mainstay for the ministry with this operation.

In addition to our own finances we also received donations to buy machines.

One year later the work was completed and we celebrated the inauguration of the workshop and at the same time, our first big farm festival.

It was clear in our minds that we should free ourselves from all bondage to financial sponsors and that this would become a ministry of faith.

We wanted to return completely to the point where God would want to have us.

So we raised the admission age to 18 years and were automatically no more a child and youth welfare institution.

On the one hand I was sad about it, because I knew the need also among young people.

On the other hand, we realized how we had been freed.

It was a feeling as if very heavy loads had fallen from us after an especially tiring year.

Now, we had only one young adolescent, whom we accepted to receive "sheltered housing".

We issued a newsletter and advertised ourselves as a financially independent Christian therapeutic facility.

We immediately received financial support from other ministries.

We learned anew: where God is, there is life and much more.

We were led into a new freedom and a peace which could not be explained by circumstances.

Deep inside us we knew: we were on the right track!

No matter how much change was going on around us, how unpredictable the future, we were on safe ground: a place the Bible calls "Rock".

Our farm was built on peaty soil.

50 years ago trenches had been dug for the water to drain off, in order to dry out the land.

The result was that the peat bog, slumped down and started to dry.

The ground was sinking and the building clearly felt the subsidence.

In places where there were no spot footings down the white sand, the floor slabs broke off and the walls developed cracks.

The result was structural instability. To handle that, you had to do repairs all the time, to shore up and pour new concrete.

However these were only repairs: the underlying cause was not resolved.

It's often like that with our spiritual life as well.

By returning to our spiritual roots, the foundation of our calling into ministry, we had found solid ground on which we could rebuild.

It was a new start with God's help.

Individuals were convinced about this decision, so coworkers applied to us, a bible school sent interns and we received strong encouragement from churches as well.

It didn't take long until we admitted our first guests in the new therapy programme.

We had the feeling we should start from scratch, despite having been in it for so long.

There were new house rules, we had a different concept and more intensive prayer times.

The spiritual programme took on a more important significance.

It was freedom through God's Spirit, which was also touched our therapy participants.

We experienced anew and much more intensely the work of God among us, with people givng their lives to Jesus and individuals experiencing visible change.

God's standards attained a new value.

The tragedy of individual cases was turned into blessings.

A young man came to us, who had recently become a father.

That was the motivation for him to get free of drugs and assume responsibility for the new-born life.

His girlfriend and child moved near to us after some time, and with God's help, he wanted to start a new life.

He made the decision to live his life with Jesus.

He went through many ups and downs, but God kept him and strengthened his personality.

He was baptized in our church.

While his life style was very chaotic, he kept to his resolution and completed the therapy with us before starting a carpentry apprenticeship with Martin.

He saw his little daughter growing up, and the relationship with his girlfriend became more stable.

So they married and moved into a small apartment in Papenburg.

He stayed with us as a trainee and switched to the co-worker team.

Through his authentic lifestyle he has become an important co-worker in our facility.

God can do that!

If we are faithful in what God entrusts to us, he will bring forth many blessings out of it.

Faithfulness is one of God's characteristics.

But he also requires faith and patience from us.

This is something he already required from his servants in the Old Testament, like Abraham (Hebrews chapter 6: verses 12-15 / Genesis chapter 15).

How often did I catch myself receiving promises from God, but waiting to see them become reality lasted too long for me, and sometimes I didn't see them accomplished at all.

Is our faith so strong that we start trying to help God out a little bit?

When I examine the therapeutic work on the farm, I quite often get into the temptation of helping things to happen a little bit here and there.

God's ways are often not my ways.

For example, let's take human feasibility, as it relates to professional competence.

Many situations mislead me into first seizing the initiative myself and then only later asking God.

It must be the other way round!

Everyone who lives on the farm, is a creation of God.

He is the one who acts and rules.

It is about the recognition of the supernatural, which is not always comprehensible; the belief in miracles, of which everyone of us represents one.

We cannot help everyone who has come or will come to us.

It is God who ultimately holds the reins.

In Psalm 107 is a Bible passage which I often quote.

It says there at the beginning:

"Oh, give thanks to the LORD, for He is good! For His mercy endures forever.

Let the redeemed of the LORD say so, Whom He has redeemed from the hand of the enemy ... We have a merciful God!"

When I turned to God at that time on the street and gave my life to him, I was anything but pious.

My condition spoke rather of neglect and of criminal energy.

Although I understood by and by, that God sets other values and standards for life, it was not possible for me to accomplish them on my own.

God spoke to my heart, a calling came deep down inside of me came into my life.

He pulled me out of misery, into a new life!

Whenever I started to work on myself in order to fulfil these expectations, which I had I set for myself, I skidded to a halt. It was a strain: in my calendar everything had to change immediately or at least very fast.

My body did not cooperate, my personality was still hurting and sick, much of what I longed for hadn't materialized yet.

Had I perceived things wrongly?

Maybe, God had not spoken to me at all?

Nevertheless, I hung in, clinging firmly to what God had given me.

Although it was not immediately visible, God transforms us at his own speed and according to his plan.

He has time!

It is not about what we think and what we desire, but it is about accepting what God gives us.

So my attitude changed, and I realise how much has happened between then and now!

20 years ago I never would have thought that one day I would work full-time in a therapy facility.

In Psalm 107, four different human types are described:

1. **People who are scattered** (verses 2-9), people who have no homeland, who go through deserts and walk along byways.

They don't find a single town where they can live!

This passage refers to the people of Israel (returned from captivity in Egypt).

In the land of Moab, Moses gets this promise for the people and gives Joshua the leadership (Deuteronomy chapter 30). The people are hungry and thirsty.

The needs of their souls have not been satisfied!

They are ruled by: loneliness, strife, fear, guilt, longing for love and acceptance.

What does God do?

He satisfies the thirsty soul and feeds the hungry one with good things!

2. **People in darkness and the shadow of death** (verses 10-16)

I.e. people in bondage.

They live under constraints and are in the hands of Satan.

Maybe they are religious, perhaps entangled in heresy, like people following other religions, or in a cult.

These are people who have been in bondage, surrounded by spiritual darkness.

Literally, it means there are shadows of death upon them.

They live in rejection, rebellion, humiliation, and they despise the counsel of God.

What does God do?

He breaks the gates of brass, and cut the bars of iron!

3. **People who are designated as fools (verses 17-22)**

These people do not listen to God although they know Him.

They rail against Him and cannot forgive.

These people are sick!

Here, the wages of sin become visible!

These people are totally unhappy.

In this Psalm it says: they are without appetite, they are no longer in a position to take in positive things.

People who are no longer capable of returning by themselves!

It is as if there is a wall around them and they can't get out of there on their own..

The leopard can no longer change his spots.

What does God do?

He delivers and heals!!! He sends his word!

That reminds me of the the centurion of Capernaum's petition (Luke 7:7):" But say the word, and my servant will be healed."

4. People on the journey (verses 23-32)

Here, traders are mentioned.

God makes Himself known through these people, at a time when there were no Scriptures, there was no Old Testament.

The merchants go from place to place telling others what God is doing.

They are the messengers of God!

They are people who are travelling with God.

They experience God's power and his miracles.

And yet, there are spiritual ups and downs among them.

They don't trust God enough.

They sin, even though they have experienced so much with him.

They want to explain God with their intellect, but they cannot!

They are afraid, in distress, despair, suffering under constant attacks.

What does God do?

God has power over the storms of our lives!

He is the eye of the storm!

All human beings have this in common: out of their distress they cry out to God!

What does God do?

God saves, God performs miracles, God blesses.

From verse 33 onwards, it is described how he helps.

God makes the impossible possible.

He is the Creator God.

He is invincible in his power.

He ultimately decides over life and death.

In his hand is everything:

drought/ floods

famine

desolate places

agriculture and harvest

descendants and earthly blessings

discipline

He conquers enemies

He protects the poor

The upright see it and are happy.

Enemies are silenced.

At the end, in verse 43, we get another very good piece of advice:

"Whoever is wise will observe these things,

And they will understand the lovingkindness of the LORD!"

When I have this Psalm before my eyes and realize every day anew, that everything, really really everything, is in God's hands, then I can do the work entrusted to me with a divine tranquillity.

No matter whether plans or finances or the precious act of "being" is involved, everything is in His hands.

Then it's much easier to cope with the situation when people discontinue their therapy or do not behave the way I would wish them to.

Then I know this wasn't a result of my failure, but rather it happened by God's permission - and this sets me free.

That helps me to establish a healthy distance from the individuals I accompany and counsel.

That sets me free to continue my way and not be bogged down by any minor details.

As we go through life understanding this, we allow ourselves to be transformed.

Again and again we think of this encouragement of God for his servants, be it Moses or Joshua (Joshua chapter 1, verse 9):

"Do not be afraid, nor be dismayed, for the LORD your God is with you wherever you go."

We must have spiritual fellowship at the centre of our ministry on the Teen Challenge project farm.

The farm is to be a spiritual centre, but equally important is our commitment towards our supporting church fellowships.

God has an army, no lone warriors.

We need a home!

If we want to make a difference in this world, we need cohesion, unity and the common goal of reaching people for Christ.

I am grateful for the many small and large congregations around us.

This is what makes God's world colourful and enriching. We are part of them with our God-given gifts and capacities and we are also strengthened to be a light in this world.

Once a year we celebrate a farm party where many Christians and non-Christians come together.

Everyone who comes wants to know this ministry better and to celebrate with us.

What an opportunity, what a testimony, when we explain what God is doing, rather than on our human activities.

The work has now been running for over 15 years and even from the outside it is easy to see the continuing ongoing changes to the farm.

Be it externally with building and structural alterations, or in the nature of the ministry with people, who are living here at that moment, it is a process being shaped by God.

We as a family are living in the thick of it and enjoy this life in spite of all its challenges.

A few years ago our farm festival motto was "Sharing Life", which is a fitting description of what we are aiming to do and which brings us great fulfilment.

Our children have grown up in this ministry. They have learned a lot and enjoyed being part of this committed community, although for sure there are also disadvantages in not having your parents for yourself in such a group context.

Of course a family also needs its private space.

For this reason, we bought a trailer for ourselves and put it on a rented site, about an hour from Hasselbrock.

We spend our days off and holidays there.

We are delighted that some of our young staff were recruited through the therapy they themselves had experienced here.

They are living testimonies of our loving God.

44. A Yes To Life

Besides the farm and our church activities we also tried to protect our private life as well as possible. That was not always easy, as we lived right next to our youths.

There were no service or working hours.

You always needed to be available on demand.

One of the consequences of this was that I was able to hide my own shortcomings and hurts well behind my work.

I was still plagued by my own beginnings, because I knew that, like a sponge with water, I had absorbed so much which I had yet to deal with.

Another long-term consequence was that I was not confident in having my own family.

Was I capable of handling a baby correctly?

So I blamed our childlessness onto the work and tried to block out my problems.

Essentially Martin desired to have children and I was often in despair, torn between "not daring" and wanting to raise a family.

As time went by there were enquiries about our "family planning" which was often a pain in the neck to us.

What was there to say about it?

It was a miracle for me when our daughter came into the world, seven years after our wedding.

I was grateful to God that he obviously had confidence in me, and here was the most amazing gift.

When our daughter was four months old we dedicated her in our congregation.

A calamity overwhelmed us in the evening of the same day.

Rebecca was in her bed and had turned blue; she had stopped breathing!

For me, my world collapsed in a moment.

Martin had the baby in his arms and called the emergency doctor; I on the other hand, raced out on the street and ran riot.

I implored God not to take this child from me.

Eventually I saw a flashing blue light in the distance as it approached me.

When the emergency doctor was finally there, our daughter was already out of being in a life-threatening condition.

I stayed a few a days in hospital with her while she underwent check-ups.

Nothing remained from that incident.

For one year she wore a monitor which controlled her breathing.

Out of concern we let her sleep in our bedroom at night.

After Rebecca, Tobias and Anna Lea came into the world two years after each other.

My pregnancy with Tobias became a real challenge.

Most of the time I had to lie down out of fear we could lose the child.

I had a lot of time for reading and writing.

I began to contemplate new concepts related to the farm.

On 8 August 1999, Tobias was born in good health in Papenburg.

All three children enrich our lives.

We cherish them and are happy that God gave them to us.

I was made more whole through them.

The remainder of my hurts and structure-bound experiences are part of an everlasting process of healing and restoration.

I am also thankful that I found people whom I allowed to speak into my life.

Through them I have experienced for myself how allowing changes, receiving criticism and encouragement all serve to move my life forward.

I can only recommend anyone to seek such people!

For a long time I took the view that a physician shouldn't become sick or a police man couldn't crash in an accident.

I didn't want to admit my own weaknesses.

Slowly it trickled into my conscience that this was the dumbest rubbish and an expression of my human pride.

Once, a good friend minted the following sentence:

'If you want to help others, you must also be ready to let others help you.'

Today I am more ready accept my weaknesses.

That makes me more approachable for many.

Of course, it is not advisable to throw your feelings and thoughts around.

It is important to develop a certain sensitivity for your environment, otherwise you might also cause some damage.

But with those people who I am close to - be it my family, my staff or also some friends - I want to stay open and be accountable.

This has clearly enriched my life.

I have found a Yes for what God loves and has created: the new life in me through Jesus.

A life intended by God, as King David already stated in Psalm 139, verses 13-14:

"For you created my inmost being; you knit me together in my mother's womb.

I praise you because I am fearfully and wonderfully made!

Your works are wonderful, I know that full well!"

It is worthwhile to read the entire Psalm, where it says among other things that God reads us.

When we are aware of this, it is often ridiculous how we behave!

He knows anyway, who we are and what we think.

Instead of using our energy to put on a very elaborate act, we could invest our energy for God!

At the end of this Psalm David states:

"Search me, O God, and know my heart; test me and know my anxious thoughts!

See if there is any offensive way in me, and lead me in the way everlasting."

45. Hatred And Forgiveness

There is nothing worse than to be burdened with unforgiven guilt.

It leads to guaranteed spiritual stagnation.

We learned through Jesus what it means to experience forgiveness and deliverance.

We are living in that year of the LORD's favour!

And that also requires us to show it in how we live.

A life pleasing to God has nothing in common with our own sense of justice nor with spiritual pride.

We have no monopoly on divinity, we are living on earth as human beings, and as long as this is our place we should behave and conduct ourselves in the way God expects of us.

In the Bible, Jesus uses parables to explain to us again and again,that we are not to judge our fellow human beings or to put our own interests in front of other's.

It is important that we let God train our characters.

When it concerns us as human beings, the Bible places the work of transforming our hearts in the centre.

God's requires us, among other things, to be holy and to be people of integrity.

In 1 Peter chapter 1, verse 15, the Old Testament is quoted:

"But just as he who called you is holy, so be holy in all you do!

For it is written:

Be holy, because I am holy."

If you want to know, what a perfect character looks like, you only need to read Galatians.

There you have it in black and white in chapter 5.

It's also clear to me that it is the greatest nonsense to take on everything in my own strength.

I can't continuously monitor myself and try to change myself.

It is important that I am open for change, so that God can mould me, whatever form that takes.

But one thing is a fact: If we let God reign, then he will also take up residence in us.

And then the Holy Spirit begins to work in us.

Through the holiness and the perfection of the one who lives in us, fruits of the Spirit will be brought forth.

These are the characteristics of a saint.

Characteristics become visible and are clear proof of God's transforming work in us.

They do not emerge overnight, but need time to mature.

I still know that it was a process for me to understand and put into practice the difference between "mine and thine".

Today it is really important for me, to be upright and honest.

I am very particular and serious about that; I can't just "turn a blind eye to it."

A basic condition for growing these fruits is a redeemed and renewed life, following a deliberate decision for Jesus.

In addition I must put aside all pride, because God can change me only if I bow to Him in humility.

It is important to know what God wants; meaning, that we remain in continuous contact with Him and his word.

Through Bible is the standard by which we can live.

In this way I also allow God to show me my shortcomings and I know that he does not want to oppress me, but to transform me through His love and patience.

Many an aspect of our negative image needs a long time to mature, just like other fruit that we eat.

It is not we, who determine how long, but God.

We must indicate our willingness that we want to work on ourselves and at the same time give God permission to correct and change us.

I always see the sins of others clearly and look down on them, just like the comparison of the speck in your neighbours' eye and the log in your own, described in the Bible.

I am responsible for my own actions and attitudes, not for those of people around me.

I don't gain anything by comparing myself with others.

Let's take the situation with my mother, my foster parents and everyone else who had any share of my life.

If I am completely honest, then I would say that the others were all guilty for my dark past.

If – then.

It feels downright good to put the blame on others, except that it doesn't belong there.

What was my share of the blame?

Weren't there enough situations where I had been the black sheep, where I had been the trigger, where I needed to ask for forgiveness.

"The others are guilty, it's their fault ..." is a knockout argument, which denies any personal accountability and willingness for personal change.

Of course, my environment has contributed to who I am.

But, ultimately it is not what happens to me which defines my life experience, but rather, what I make out of it.

Each hurt, each injury which shaped my life also opened up opportunities for me to learn something new on a personal level.

It can be compared with physical fractures and injuries.

At the point where a bone is sprained or broken it will grow cartilage and particularly solid tissue, and it probably won't break again at this spot. Even concerning us humans it is argued that a bone would break twice at the same spot.

The parts where we are injured can become our strongest points, providing we receive the right treatment.

As a plant needs an experienced gardener and a person needs a good doctor, so God wants to be our healer and to nurture us.

The first step in the right direction is to allow God to deal with me.

Sometimes, this can be tremendously painful, when old scabs break open, and the whole misery and all the hurt becomes visible again.

Air gets at the wound and you might want to hold your breath and even cry aloud:

"I cannot bear this!" Then God starts to disinfect and remove all the bad germs and treat the wound so that the healing process can begin.

It was exactly like that with me, and what pain, rage and hate surfaced, when I allowed God to deal with these old hurts.

I would have loved to escape from myself.

I cannot deny that I have nursed abysmal thoughts in my mind, and was more than once on the verge of throwing my life away.

But it is also good to know that you cannot fall deeper than into God's hands, if you are his child.

I know that I can't run away.

Bettina will have this mirror, reflecting her own personality, facing her everywhere she goes!

Of course, God loves me as I am.

He also does not cease to love me, if I stay the way I am.

But he can't bless me as he wants to, if I am not prepared to allow changes to who I am, if I do not take steps to forgive and respond to hurts with the love of Jesus.

I should constantly remember how much God has forgiven me.

In the Epistle of Colossians, chapter 3, verse 13 it says:

"Bear with each other and forgive whatever grievances you may have against one another. Forgive as the Lord forgave you!"

Of course, I could argue that in my situation, these weren't people who knew God and they didn't even show they were ready to receive forgiveness.

But that is not the point.

God's call is universally valid: forgive!

God loves me too much to leave me as I am.

I needed a lot of time until this process, of having my attitude transformed, led to me being able to put it into practice in my life.

It became possible with my foster parents, when I started my street ministry in the Lower Rhine region.

Our relationship never became affectionate, but it was harmonious.

So they accepted my ways, even if they couldn't understand me.

Of course, our opposing views clashed repeatedly, but we became good dispute-partners and gradually our ability to manage conflicts matured.

One first highlight was the time when my foster father and I went on a tour in the Bernese Oberland; it was the first time that I had no problems addressing him as "father".

A few months later he enrolled at the Open University in Hagen, and we were fellow students.

He began to study law and modern history.

It was fun to talk shop with him and sometimes we unconsciously excluded those around us.

There was healing!

I started to like him very much, and for me it was a heavy blow, when one day I got the news that he was suffering from bone cancer.

It was already in an advanced stage.

I freed myself up from my duties at home as much as I was able, so that I could visit and care for him.

For the first time in my life it struck me how very difficult it can be to say a proper goodbye.

All at once I needed to catch up on so many things.

But time was running out!

We talked about faith, about eternity, and also about the past and of my own experience with cancer and how God had healed me.

He prayed to Jesus at the side of his deathbed.

The relationship towards my foster mother, however, only improved very slowly.

She remained "only" the foster mother, and I could not simply accept her.

What did change was my attitude.

I tried to meet her in an accommodating and friendly way.

When she needed help I volunteered, and she started to visit us, even though she carried on proving how little she understood of our lifestyle with faith at its centre.

She lived her own life and I had to leave it at that.

I knew it was such a great sacrifice for her when she condescended to our level.

Little by little we found a common level of communication.

The most difficult challenge was the relationship with my birth-mother.

If I'm honest, it is rather one-sided, in my view.

I still love her very much, and my greatest desire would be for her to smile at me.

Instead I receive something which ranges from apathy to rejection.

I regularly went to visit her and each time I reached Reeperbahn station on the S1 train, my heart was beating in somersaults.

It was still home to me and no matter what brokenness I found there, it was nonetheless a part of me.

In the past when I was very young in my faith, I was often embarrassed to be seen coming from that neighbourhood.

Today, I am disgusted by the environment, but I also feel a sense of love and compassion.

The people here are loved by God!

How glad I am that the Salvation Army has a base here and that they maintain contact with people.

Me too, I was also released from this milieu through their help!

When I went along the dirty passage to my mother's home, it was guaranteed I would have to stumble through liquor bottles and trash.

If I was unlucky, I would be accosted by someone who was half-drunk.

At the top of the house I came to a darkened apartment where my mother worked and lived.

A haze of alcohol and sweat greeted everyone who came in.

In one room was a sofa in the Art Nouveau style, where she often sat, stony-faced.

She would be taking cocaine and drinking.

Arguably it could be said that I had seldom seen her sober.

Her old men could be jumping around her, and despite her condition she still seemed to control everything.

Next to the bar below was her apartment, a chic style of sleazy hotel. People would go in and out incognito, after spending a lot of money.

How many times had I spoken to her and been met with a vacant gaze? She ignored me or told me to work for her, but she never looked at me with the eyes that I longed for.

It's so sad that I also had to know her hateful, brutal side.

As often as I could, I told her about Jesus.

I have forgiven her and what remains is still a longing for love, and unfortunately, also a lot of stress and anxiety.

One day when I was back in Hamburg, I discovered that minors were working in her bar.

I was shocked, and my first reaction was to threaten to report it.

I already knew of certain websites, mobile brothels and private clubs and now I was fully convinced that I had to do something.

Out of sheer determination I brought some of my mother's pimps and sympathizers into the arena.

It ended with me receiving terrible threats, but I knew my life was in God's hands.

However, for my family and their protection, I needed some more faith.

Sometimes I find myself overwhelmed by fear and I want to protect my children especially, and yet I cannot.

But I do know that God is with us as a family.

Our family is a gift from God!

After so many years of living with God, for me it was a very traumatic situation which then ensued.

Everybody had left the farm, except my kids who were already in bed.

It was just before Christmas.

Late in the evening a car arrived on the farm, and the house door opened.

I was expecting Martin, as he was due back from a Christmas party.

Not suspecting anything, I was sitting in the living room, when three men entered the room.

I knew the one from Hamburg.

He was known as a bully boy.

They threatened me and raped me, and I was in shock.

I panicked, thinking: "What will happen to my children?"

In fact, they even threatened to bring them out of their bedrooms.

Willingly I did everything that was asked of me.

It was absolutely humiliating.

I don't know how long their visit lasted, it seemed like an eternity to me.

When they had left, I was shaking all over.

I registered only fear.

When Martin finally got home, I was lying in bed, exhausted.

I tried to explain what had happened to him.

For me it caused a deep emotional and physical injury that still returns today in so-called flashbacks.

I am certain that I will and must continue to be willing to forgive my mother and her assistants.

It is not always easy but I know that, with God, I don't have another alternative.

Ultimately, I myself am living by the grace of God.

Now that the distance between my mother and me is less (contact between us is more frequent), I also realise how hurt I am, being the child.

But ultimately I am following Jesus, have received a clear calling from God and I want to remain faithful to what God has called me.

Faithfulness is a trait which God mentions in the Bible.

This is written in James, chapter 5, verse 12:

"But let your "Yes," be "Yes," and your "No," "No."

For me that means: to stand by my words, and to stand by other people, even in times of conflict and to follow the call of God, stand in his service and not run away at the first sign of difficulty.

So it is my call to do missionary work at Teen Challenge and not on the Reeperbahn.

46. On The Way

When I look back, God's work and dealings with me at various stages of my life can be seen like a scarlet thread.

At the beginning He gave me life -and it was no accident, and then came many life experiences, which He has transformed for good up to this day.

This is God's wise preparation.

He is without time, and sometimes I feel knowing that to be very reassuring.

God knows yesterday, today and tomorrow, and I do not need to worry about anything!

To be with God on the way, means to run in the track that he provides.

This is not always the easiest path, and I contend that sometimes it seemed totally unnecessary "to only rely on God", rather than to take my life into my own hands.

As Christians, we live a life under guidance!

We can organize our mental life on more than one level simultaneously.

On one level we think, talk, see, calculate and fulfil all outward requirements.

But on another level within us, we can pray, sing, praise and be receptive to the breath of God.

(quote by T. Kelly) We are on one level when we talk to God, but we are on another level when we listen to Him.

When we listen to God, the Holy Spirit works in us.

I am very open to the possibility that God speaks directly to me.

I am convinced that God offers each of us this guidance, if our relationship with him is right. I have received visions from him and usually saw them become reality soon after.

The fact that my actions and longing may be out of step with God's timing, is something I have often misunderstood.

Then it is as if someone has had to pull the emergency brake.

At this point, it is not easy to maintain our balance.

In 2 Corinthians, chapter 10, verse 5 it is written:

"We ... take captive every thought to make it obedient to Christ."

It can hurt when you missed the exit and have to make a massive detour.

I experienced this a few times in my ministry with Teen Challenge.

I have a vision to build a meeting place in Hasselbrock; a place which promotes wellbeing and refreshment.

To accomplish this we need people who support the ministry, pillars on which the whole thing rests.

In addition to having therapists it means having a stable team that assists on a voluntary basis.

My vision for this project has taken a new lease of energy each time I have been able to recruit people.

Unfortunately, it then often happens that I overwhelm these people, so that they pull back from the ministry, even before they had begun.

Training, releasing, searching afresh: this drains our strength and breaks the momentum of the whole process.

Again and again I had to change plans (and change my attitude), acknowledging the will of God in this project ahead of my own plans and desires.

This brought me to a place of personal brokenness.

I have become more cautious, learning to let staff settle and allowing them to find their feet in ministry.

Nevertheless I want to explain the clear path which God promised me.

At the beginning of the trail was the vision set out in Isaiah chapter 61.

Hasselbrock was the place chosen for the vision to become reality, with God determining the schedule and time.

It was important for us not just to sit back and take things easy, but to keep going.

So we have expanded the number of places available for people to have therapy treatment, offered training for employees and conducted seminars again and again.

We invite ourselves into churches, because this is an important element of our ministry.

We see ourselves as assisting the churches and want to use our professional qualifications to offer help. Naturally this partnership benefits both parties: we assist the churches, while at the same time recognising that we could not exist without their support.

We need the community of believers: we need to commit to fellowship with the Body of Jesus.

Anyone who works in such a ministry should be consistent in this area.

For our team it is a must so that we can cooperate strategically and not duplicate one another's efforts.

Paul, Silvanus and Timothy wrote a letter to the church of Thessalonica. In 1 Thessalonians chapter 2 verse 8 they wrote the following sentence:

"We loved you so much that we were delighted to share with you not only the gospel of God but our lives as well, because you had become so dear to us."

There are several ways to work within the congregation.

You can invest your gifts and talents, provide your professional knowledge - and that is certainly also an important task- but you can also invest yourself, at the same time as providing your gifts, just as these three men describe in the Epistle to the Thessalonians.

What we do in our ministry as Teen Challenge staff, does not only mean that we invest our gifts but that we employ our whole lives.

It means not only showing compassion as we visit people and offering help without thinking of our own interests, but it also means dedicating ourselves completely.

As I share my heart with the group on the farm and with my own congregation, I need to be sensitive to their pain and help to carry their loads, and in this way I can share their failures, successes and also their inmost pain and personal experience of faith.

I have experienced how my relationship with the church strengthens me, particularly in the area of spiritual growth, which goes on to impact the ministry of the farm project.

Ultimately it is a merging of ministry and church into one "family".

The question is whether we will only invest our gifts or whether we are willing to invest our whole selves?

Do we content ourselves with only fulfilling a task or do we desire to invest our lives?

For me, being a disciple means doing the will of the Father in Heaven, regardless of how popular it makes me with others.

My calling is to this therapeutic facility, until God shows me otherwise, no matter how I am feeling. Not everything always goes smoothly, as we are way too human, but still the confirmation of my calling is there:

"The Spirit of the Lord is upon me." (Isaiah 61:1)

I am particularly grateful for our young co-workers!

I desire for them to be certain of God's plan for their lives.

God wants to use our life experiences for a good purpose.

In my heart I feel so grateful.

Without God I would be lost; probably I would not be alive any more.

I would not have experienced salvation from my guilt and sin.

This gratitude has saved me from making many stupid choices.

Many claim, if they could turn back time, they would do many things differently.

I strongly doubt this!

Without God, nothing would run as one thinks.

47. Companions Along The Way

I am thankful for those people who have to some extent accompanied my life.

Right now I would like to express my gratitude to my foster parents, without whom I certainly would not be where I am now.

They accepted me as their child, although I never wanted to be.

They fostered and raised me, often without receiving a word of thanks!

On the contrary, they endured a lot of pain and still supported me.

I abandoned them in their pain and sorrow, and yet they accepted me again.

Today I am deeply embarrassed about it, and I am glad that God's grace brought healing here!

I am thankful that they were always there for my children, that they have loved und provided for them, in any way they could. (My foster father died in 1998)

My prayer for them is:

"I hope and pray that you would get to know Jesus Christ as your personal Lord and Saviour!

He also knows all the bitterness in your heart and would like to liberate you."

I thank my friend and brother who pursued me and led me to believe, even though I made terrible threats! He was the messenger of God, who was on the road in Jesus' name. May God bless him in his ministry. Through him and the former team of the New Life Tea Room, I had the chance for a new beginning. Although I have also disappointed him, he supported me and stood by my side. Thank you a lot!

Then I should mention:

My friends- who helped me to go through the valleys and to enjoy the heights, those who were with me when I was sick and who supported me in prayer. Very often you stood in the gap and pleaded for me. God bless you!

Martin's family - through whom I discovered family life. They accepted me as I was, and included me in their lives. That means a lot to me, and I love them.

Martin - you have stood by my side, even though you knew that it would not be easy to deal with me. You have accepted me and supported me. My aloofness and my deep hurts have not stopped you from loving me. You are God's greatest gift. Thank you for your love and patience, which helps me to stay on the path.

Our children, as well, have made my life more valuable. I am very thankful to God that we may accompany Rebecca, Tobias and Anna Lea a bit and enjoy them.

Thank you Lord, that you have enabled me as a mother to provide for my children and to parent them.

My teachers and mentors - I have learned a lot from you and have always been able to ask for advice (even if you were far away).

Teen Challenge is my place, where God has called me to be since finishing Bible School. It is my spiritual family, in which I feel very comfortable. Here I have many valuable people around me, colourful and international, and each of them has made my life richer through their character.

Martin and I got engaged and also married at Teen Challenge. This worldwide Christian organization has become my home.

Thank you, leaders – for accepting me in your circle! For many years we have stood together, praying and striving for one goal: to give a home to people who have no home, and to reach out to them for Christ.

My heart belongs to the Teen Challenge House Project in Hasselbrock, where I live and work.

I thank God for this ministry! It is beautiful to see it grow and being supplied. It's great to live in one location with so many precious people. Every day I learn more about living an authentic life and you are my mirror. I am privileged to have walked a part of life's road together with everyone who has lived or is living here, and to grow to know them better. As you let me look into your lives, thank you for your trust which honours me.

You dear staff, should be aware of how you are the blessing of God, even when you go through difficult times in ministry. Your reward is in heaven. If you persevere, God will reward you!

But what would the ministry be without church! Thanks to all the congregations who sponsor us and support us spiritually. Thank you for all the personal contacts. A particular thanks goes to my church which has put up with me week by week, and where I can also let myself go at times, when I need to.

Thank you also to all the people here, whom I have given permission to speak into my life.

It is a great help and I have learned to endure and accept correction in love.

One phrase has shaped me in particular:
"Those who want to help others must also be willing to be helped!"

48. Miracles Happen Again And Again

When we returned to our roots, the character of the ministry changed dramatically.

Suddenly we were dependent on God and that is better than any regular salary!

You have the opportunity to tell of God's provision and miracles; testimonies of God's omnipotence and people find themselves infected by our enthusiasm for God..

These testimonies motivate the guests and even ourselves to continue going down this path.

Of course, the greatest miracles are those of people restored by God.

Again and again I encourage our guests (patients), to testify in public of what God has done in their lives.

Not only because it is good and important for their own spiritual development, but also to give glory to God.

We thus proclaim the unchangeable reality of God.

Miracles are commonplace, when we align ourselves to God.

I think of the time when we found ourselves in a difficult situation with too few vehicles for the number of people living on the farm.

We were limited in getting around.

We literally had to vote each time: Who gets to drive and who has to stay here?

In the long term this was not a good situation, however, we weren't able to simply buy another car.

So we started to pray regularly about this need.

The first thing that happened was the transfer of a substantial donation, designated: "car".

However, this amount was not enough to buy a mini-bus.

One of our housemates was always praying for a blue bus, because it would match the rest of our car pool.

Even though I often countered that it didn't matter how the car looked, he insisted on it and prayed specifically for this day by day.

Some weeks later, the miracle happened.

We were offered a used blue Volkswagen bus, which would cost around the amount we had gathered in donations.

Two weeks later, the miracle car arrived on our farm.

Another testimony of God's power was the purchase of our new heating system.

For many years we had heated with oil.

Energy prices rose rapidly and we seriously considered whether we should switch to wood.

We had a pile of cut-offs from the workshop as well as a lot of wood to be sawn up.

As we investigated prices, it soon became clear that the total price would amount to 15,000 Euros.

For us it was an unaffordable sum.

Following our daily Bible study we have a 30 minute prayer time.

We take advantage of this to pray through our concerns, and the heating was one of them.

For weeks nothing happened and Martin decided to call a company and place an order.

I was somehow astonished about it, maybe even appalled.

You couldn't buy something without having the money!

That just showed my lack of trust and I was amazed how confident Martin appeared. In faith he expressed that it was time for the heating system to be replaced, and he had peace about it.

Just minutes after the call someone phoned us.

I almost dropped the receiver!

There was someone on the line who wanted to transfer a large sum of money to us.

I couldn't believe it at first.

Then it simply bubbled out of me and I told the donor that Martin had just bought a heating system.

This person found it a reasonable investment and promised to transfer the remainder needed within the next months to us.

These are miracles!

This person had known nothing of our plans, and God used him.

So the Lord is our provider at the Project Farm.

We are learning day by day not to lose confidence, as it brings great rewards!

In addition, the blessing is often so abundant, that many others can benefit too.

For instance we regularly receive donations from a Dutch food bank.

Sometimes it is such a plethora of food that we ourselves are able to share with needy families.

49. Purpose Driven Life

While the title of this book is "Set Into Life" it also has to do with a purpose, a divine plan that is behind our lives.

My birth wasn't of my own doing: it was merely in God's hand.

God was still there when I took over responsibility for my life.

While he let me have my freedom and permitted many things to happen that were not according to his will, He never left me.

Every once in a while, at various stages of life, I met him.

And then there was the definite point when I turned back to him.

At that moment, I was filled with a deep gratitude, which has never left me.

It was important, yes, it became priority in my life to follow Jesus, to ask: "Where is my calling?"

I had to make certain that I was where God wanted me to be and I longed to put God's instructions into practice, letting the visions I received, become reality; pictures, dreams, thoughts that did not originate from myself.

The farm is such a vision, but it is expandable.

This is what God can do with a life, when we stay close to Him. We need to make staying online with him a principle for our lives.

This is the only way to know which plans and goals God has with you and through you.

Visions for work and for us individually are important, as they are the impetus which propels us.

Life with God is not at a standstill, but is a race with a goal.

In Philippians, Paul writes:

"Not that I have already attained, or am already perfected; but I press on, that I may lay hold of that for which Christ Jesus has also laid hold of me.

Brethren, I do not count myself to have apprehended.

But one thing I say:

I forget those things which are behind and reach forward to those things which are ahead, I press toward the goal for the prize of the upward call of God in Christ Jesus." (Philippians 3:12-14)

God's timelessness is difficult for us human beings to understand.

He sees us from the beginning; from our inception in the womb until our dying day here on earth.

For him, nothing in our lives is a surprise.

He knows from the outset that our lives matter.

The visions we get for our lives, are a part of his plan.

They may be single milestones, or perhaps carry us for a period of time.

As long as I am here on this earth, I will seek God's voice and reach forward to those things which are ahead, the prize of the upward call of God.

There is no better goal to aim towards.

Nothing on earth is more valuable or deserves more attention and energy from us.

Again and again we need to be aware that we can't take our lives with us when we go. Nothing we build and accomplish here will serve us for eternity.

Our lives are to be concerned with God's plans for this world, and we are his tools.

Our only responsibility is to serve him.

My path led me to Teen Challenge.

There is a clear calling on my life and yet it is important to listen every day anew to what God plans to do.

We can't be too sure, that once in a while, God won't change his instructions.

While I was serving in that café ministry, I suddenly became completely certain, that my time there was up.

God spoke, lit a beacon and showed me through other people what he intended to do next.

It is important not to take any decisions in isolation, but to watch out for how God confirms a change of course in different ways.

It is dangerous to take a decision in a momentary situation without confirmation from several sides.

Our home church performs an important function at this point.

God appoints spiritual leadership as a general principle.

In 1 Thessalonians it is written:

"But we request of you, brethren, that you appreciate those who diligently labour among you, and have charge over you in the Lord and give you instruction, and that you esteem them very highly in love because of their work. Live in peace with one another."(1Thessalonians 5:12-13)

It is absolutely biblical to share my thoughts, visions and calling with the church leadership and ask them to consider them with discernment.

In doing so I stay on the safe side.

When we wanted to start the ministry on the farm, we consulted with the elders and Martin's parents and asked them to pray over it.

Their perspective was important, and confirmed what we felt God had spoken to us.

Discernment is vital in ascertaining if something is really from God.

Not my ideas, not my plans, but the trust in God's promises and his plan makes visions sustainable.

Several verses further on in 1Thessalonians chapter 5 verses 19-22 we read:

"Do not quench the Spirit; do not despise prophetic utterances. But examine everything carefully.

Hold fast to that which is good; abstain from every form of evil!

When we started the project Back to the Roots, we consulted with the pastor of our congregation.

We also asked the board of our social ministry to give us the green light. Through everything we experienced with God we know that it has been the right way.

God has confirmed our course.

In the meantime many people passed through our institution.

I claim that God left his marks on everybody.

Some only stayed for a short time or dropped out. Yet, it is exactly these men in whom I am very sure that God sowed a seed.

Those people who got started and continued their walk with God after therapy, are men in which faith was roused by the Word of God.

Through that they became strengthened in their personalities, so much so, that they can be a testimony to others through their deeds.

These are men, who will build the Kingdom of God with others, be it in mission ministry abroad, in church ministry or in a rehabilitation institution.

They are the mouthpiece of the message of salvation in this world.

When I look back, I am happy because I know that God placed me at the right spot.

Multiplication is the fruit that is produced when we are living according to the will of God.

Therefore, I can only encourage every visionary.

Seek people who support you on your path, who accompany you and who can speak into your life:

"Never walk alone!"

Thinking about Teen Challenge Project Farm in Hasselbrock, I know that God still has so many plans.

More and more, I see the picture of a spiritual centre before my eyes, the outfitting of the barn, the people who will find a home here.

Repeatedly we, the Teen Challenge leadership team, had the vision of an ark.

Is that what is to be here?

Far away in the countryside, still further away from churches.

Will a church one day be established nearby - a church fellowship offering a spiritual home for the people entrusted to us?

I am willing to be led and guided by God.

This year we have started collecting for the outfitting of the barn.

Yet, despite still waiting for the financial blessing, we have instead received many material donations.

This is God! He has his plans.

My expectations were completely different.

Life with God keeps being exciting.

When I am invited anywhere to give an account of the ministry, it all overflows out of me, because we have experienced an abundance of miracles throughout this journey.

Increasingly, we are going on outreaches to congregations to tell them about the ministry. We as a team from TC Project Farm know very well that, as well as sharing the living testimonies of the people in therapy, we want to impact people with the Great Commission of God.

Go therefore, do not stop sharing the Good News of Salvation for humanity through Jesus Christ with people!

And then I often have the grave of Evi before my eyes.

It is my memorial.

This human being never consciously claimed God's love for herself.

Out of desperation for her situation she wished death for herself and jumped out of a window.

Had she known of Jesus?

Had anyone told her the glad tidings of forgiveness, grace and a life worth living with God?

I don't know. But I know about the importance of the ambassadors in the court of hell, without whom I wouldn't now be in full-time ministry for God, but would have succumbed to my previous lifestyle.

50. Grace Prospect

"It is for freedom that Christ has set us free. Stand firm, then, and do not let yourselves be burdened again by a yoke of slavery." (Galatians chapter 5, verse 1)

Through faith in Jesus Christ we have been set free.

When Paul wrote his Letter to the Galatians, he chose the theme "Redemption by Grace."

We read in all 6 chapters that we have been saved by faith, and the Spirit of God wants to work in us in order to bring forth good fruit.

In the last chapter, Paul particularly emphasizes that we should keep an eye on one another.

But we must recognise that this freedom, which we have obtained, is a gift!

There is nothing we can add to it.

"Only faith gives us divine power to obtain the fruits of the Spirit.

But the fruit of the Spirit is love, joy, peace, patience, kindness, goodness, faithfulness, gentleness and self-control. Against such things there is no law. Those who belong to Christ Jesus have crucified the sinful nature with its passions and desires." (Galatians 5:22-24)

And first of all comes the power of forgiveness!

Everybody experiences this in their life, as they bring their old life before God.

As Jesus preaches the Sermon on the Mount, he describes for us what it means to live this power of forgiveness.

This is not a one-time procedure, but a lifestyle.

In Matthew chapter 5, verses 44-45 Jesus says these words:

"But I say to you,

love your enemies!

Bless those who curse you, do good to those who hate you.

Pray for those who spitefully use you and persecute you!

That you may be children of your heavenly Father."

According to these words we cannot choose whom to forgive.

Jesus emphasises that no matter how deeply we have been hurt, we are to forgive.

Jesus says so in verse 46:

"For if you love those who love you, what recompense will you have?

Do not the tax collectors do the same?"

So it doesn't matter who has angered or hurt me.

A lifestyle of forgiveness needs to be fully embraced if we don't want get robbed of our blessing!

In Matthew chapter 6 verses 14-15 Jesus says:

"For if you forgive those who have who have done evil to you, your heavenly Father will also forgive you.

But if you refuse to forgive others, your Father will not forgive your sins."

This has to do with repentance and turning our lives around.

If we keep something back or bear something against someone else and are not ready to forgive, we are lacking repentance and bitterness emerges.

Out of this results spiritual emaciation, weakness and loss of faith.

I experienced myself what it means to be unreconciled.

This doesn't only have an effect on us, but on everybody else in our environment.

For a long time I was not clear about the context of forgiveness and spiritual living.

I received good teaching about it at the bible school, but it was only after I had been a Christian for many years, that I really understood the meaning of forgiveness and was able to apply it in my life.

In 2003 I began, little by little, to deal with the old issues in my "basement" and to come to terms with the past, through the help of friends and at the same time I prayed that God would fill the gaps which I had discovered.

But then it came to forgiveness!

That was hard, but even there, God gave me strength.

I understood at once: you can't earn God's forgiveness.

Only the shed blood of Jesus, that alone, has paid for the forgiveness of sins.

If I confess my sins, bringing my old issues to God, God also requires that me to forgive others.

In Colossians chapter 3, verse 13 Paul writes:

"... bearing with one another's faults, and forgiving those who hurt you.

Do not forget, even as Christ forgave you, so you also must do."

Here the instruction is about bearing with people and forgiveness.

I had to learn and understand that forgiveness is a matter of the heart and cannot be mastered by the mind.

I started to pray for my enemies, for the people who were a threat to my life and to my family members' lives.

Through this I received deliverance and power; I was delivered from pain and no longer felt the need to defend myself.

The blessing of God began to flow.

I felt it in me and in my environment: God was at work and gave me a spiritual boost.

God's mercy and grace are sufficient hour by hour, if I trust that his willingness to forgive is greater than my willingness to confess sins.

I firmly want to leave the things of the past behind - all my mistakes and sins - and to start every day anew. Living as a Christian means living out of grace. And with this lifestyle I am able to meet the many people, who God sends my way, with love.

Yet again I see how quick we are to judge and condemn!

There is a great danger of us condemning people and becoming legalistic, just like the Pharisees in the New Testament.

So easily we can adopt pious habits and give an outward show of living a holy lifestyle, while not being able and willing to acknowledge that the beam in our own eyes is greater than the mote in the eye of someone else.

As I started to understand that we still have dormant "baggage" within us, even after so many years of being a Christian, I knew in my heart that many people need help to open up and allow God to cleanse and heal their innermost secrets and hurts.

One logical consequence of this was that I started a psycho-therapy training.

Once again, God provided wonderfully.

My mentors were superb, professionally speaking and I really learned a lot from them, about seeing the desires and needs of people from a different perspective.

They don't just need food and a home, but also appreciation and respect.

They need someone who will share their visions, their experiences and their feelings and accompany them on life's way until they know for themselves, that they have found a new and good direction.

In the end I also got to know a totally different side of myself through this training.

For many years I had shied away from wearing skirts and dresses, from dressing in a feminine way, or caring about looking nice for others.

Because of my previous lifestyle I had an internal blockage and swung like a pendulum from one extreme to the other.

I went overboard to not exhibit my body for anyone.

In the end, I didn't know how to dress fashionably and it was hard for me to go shopping. I packed up and went home if the first pair of trousers I liked, didn't fit.

After the second year of training I approached a few seminar colleagues and asked them to go shopping with me.

My outlook had changed.

Now, I aim to align my outward appearance with my internal values....another step in restoring Bettina!

I have come to realize and experience that we are in a life-long continual process of change.

The training also challenged me mentally, and I noticed how much fun it was to work on specialized subjects with my seminar colleagues. I make a habit of putting my personal experience with God at the centre of all I do.

God wants to use that, and he has prepared the ground, placing the right people at my side.

My decision to start a secular training gives me the opportunity to serve this world as a believer and be acknowledged by the state.

I know that it also gives me an opportunity to help many Christians who are locked in stalemate because they have not yet grasped their share of the power for forgiveness.

In the summer of 2006 I started to develop a Christian counselling centre in Weener where they are planning to install a social network in the parish hall of Christ Church, Weener. (Christuskirche Weener).

The plan is to develop an active street ministry and to care for distressed people, alongside the provision of counselling, outpatient therapy and the organisation of placements to assisting those needing inpatient care.

This is another milestone in my life.

A life, set and determined by God!

I am grateful that God alone has everything in his hands, and that I can let myself sink into his hands without ruffle or excitement.

Joshua, the successor of Moses, received a promise from God:

"No-one will be able to stand up against you all the days of your life. As I was with Moses, so I will be with you; I will never leave you nor forsake you.

Be strong and courageous!" (Joshua 1:5-6)

I claim this promise for my life also.

God reinforces his commitment once again in verse 9 of the same chapter.

He spoke to Joshua:

"Have I not commanded you be strong and courageous?

Do not be terrified; do not be discouraged, for the LORD your God will be with you wherever you go."

Sometimes God repeats himself to show the importance of what He is saying!

I often read these verses, and they are promises which bring comfort to me. Nevertheless, the hum-drum of daily life we so often switch off to God's speaking.

This is why God reminds us again and again.

Whenever some dear fellow-believers observed that these promises had receded into the distance for me, they repeated these verses to me, to remind me of God's commitment.

Everything which God has placed into our lives is given to us, for us to share generously.

We are vessels of earth filled with the abundance of God!

Let the Spirit of God flow from you and contribute to the bringing in of a bountiful harvest.

My desire is that this book will motivate you to follow the Great Commission of God, your destiny and that you can enjoy this "life of adventure" with God, your Lord!

Nothing is more worthy than investing your life for God.

Do not be an egoist!

Share with others what you have experienced with God and live your faith authentically.

Overcome your fear of man and align yourself to God, so you will live in awe of Him.

You won't take along anything from this world.

One day you will definitely stand before Jesus, and your life will be shown for what it is.

And be assured, it does not matter where you come from and what you experienced and did.

Your choices, how you are deliberately walking with Jesus, is the essence that matters!

Jesus Christ is the one who connects us, and that counts much more.

He is the Way, the Truth and the Life.

When we are on a journey with him, we can be assured, that he will go ahead and lead us safely to where he wants us to be.

As children of God it matters that we are his people and are assembled by God as an army.

It what we have in common that matters, not what our differences are.

He is the Way!

Today it is my greatest desire that as many people as possible will experience this truth and undergo a radical change of course in their lives.

You and I can make this possible.

We can do our bit by learning from John chapter 3, verse 30:

"He must increase, but I must decrease!"

In other words:

Do not look unto yourself, do not look for benefits for yourself, but look unto Jesus, that he will be exalted.

To Him be all the glory.

He gave everything for you, and you should give every area of your life to Him.

This will enrich you!

Amen!

51. My Thoughts On Globality Or: The "Wind Of The Lord"

In conclusion I would like to share with you, my reader, what God has given to me, and what has made my relationship with him particularly precious.

I would like to take you to another dimension of this relationship.

It is an image which illustrates what it means to live out the freedom of God:

It is the image of the seagull and the wind.

Let us imagine a gull by the sea.

High above us she flies in circles.

And now, put yourself in this bird's shoes.

Maybe it is even good to close our eyes for a moment and let this image become alive in our imagination.

Imagine living in such an open space, high in the sky, being wafted by the wind.

How good that wind is, for every part of the body.

It brings freedom, expanse, overview.

I can pause and let the wind determine my direction.

I can cruise, and carried by the wind, rest on it, as far as the air current allows.

When I leave that air current flow, flying becomes very arduous.

It takes a lot of strength and becomes dangerous.

Suddenly, you might fall through a wind pocket, or you are pulled by an air vortex.

Then the freedom, orientation and enjoyment are over.

It takes a lot of strength and is dangerous.

But the gull decides for herself!

It is simple and natural.

For now it requires guts to draw strength and take advantage of the wind capacity.

I am fully aware of myself (and I am astonished about all that what is coming out).

Cautiously and bit by bit, I start to look around myself.

I succeed and feel that I have been set free; I can be totally relaxed.

With this attitude, at one with myself and my environment, using the strength provided, there is no status quo.

- And then I think of the word 'Ebenezer' ("thus far has the Lord helped me"), and my thoughts say very clearly: "No, this is not the end of the line. It goes on further."

We are on the way, nothing is complete and ready to be ticked off the list.

The wind is a continuous stream; there is life, progress, an unending process.

Wind is the air that positions us, by which we are shaped and our surroundings are influenced and which carries important things.

It is the air, the oxygen, we inhale, which lets us sense that we are alive.

The wind can be powerful, gentle, cold and warm.

And then I think of the importance of the wind, which surrounds us day by day, our whole life.

The wind serves as a means of reproduction as it carries the seed to the ends of the earth.

It controls the clouds and is responsible for rain and drought.

Wind moves soil, bears it away and creates new landscapes.

The wind enables us to view landscapes, small and isolated or in vast in area.

And then look away from you and from all you feel of the wind.

The human being takes on the power and energy of the wind.

Through him there has been technical progress.

Through him nature is being artificially altered.

But then also realize: the wind also escapes again and again.

In the end, we human beings cannot dominate the wind.

It dominates us!

It is global and ever changing.

It is the means through which our needs are met; it gives us protection and can become a risk if underestimated.

Good and evil, meekness and power lie close together.

It requires the right balance of sensitivity in how we deal with it

- And then link it with the globality of our thinking.

One thing is for sure:

There is Someone who created the wind, who holds the world in his hand; and he says:

"It is good!" If our relationship with the creator is right, then it also defines the relationship with what he created, and we are able to enjoy it, use it, admire it and let it serve us.

The wind is global, uncontainable.

God's perspective for the human being is global and also uncontainable.

It is good to again become aware of it and integrate this knowledge into our behaviour and thinking.

Then the following phrase is also true:

Unto the ends of the earth!

We can get carried off like the seagull, high in the sky.

We won't require any physical effort, simply courage and trust, and then it remains simple and natural.

From Genesis to the book of Revelations by John, the wind plays an important role in the Word of God, the bible.

Those experiences and encounters with my Lord and God changed my relationship with him a lot.

For me, living with him became something truly natural.

I do not need to ponder whether I want to have contact, it is there.

Living by faith means that I put my trust in the One who carries me, even through all the whirlwinds.

It is the most important thing I have to keep in mind:

It is precious and most of all natural providing you do not break out of this intimate relationship.

Habakkuk (a Minor Prophet in the Old Testament) wrote in his book, as he envisioned the end of the world:

"His glory covers the heavens and his praise fills the earth.

His splendour is like the sunrise; rays flash from his hand, where his power is hidden."

(Habakkuk 3:3-4) and further on:

"Yet I will rejoice in the LORD, I will be joyful in God my Saviour!

The LORD is my strength; he makes my feet like the feet of a deer, he enables me to go on the heights!"

(Habakkuk 3:18-19)

The book of Habakkuk is full of his intimate relationship with his God.

While he can hardly bear what God reveals to him, he still can stand in his open space, in meeting God.

Anything else stays behind it.

Everything around him might fall apart, yet he is firmly anchored in the relationship with his God.

God gave it to him, because Habakkuk put his confidence and faith in him.

Indeed, he surrendered himself into his hands knowing that it is good and right.

A little earlier, in Habakkuk 2:4, he already stated:

"The just shall live by his faith."

This faith and surrender make it possible to know that you are carried by the wind of the Lord even while under great strain.

That almost renders the question for the how, why, and what, redundant.

It is important that you dwell in that intimate relationship with God.

Then you are also able to bear defeats and calamities.

Then you also learn to understand Job, who, in spite of the calamities, held onto God knowing:

"The LORD gave everything to me, and the LORD has taken away everything from me.

Blessed be the name of the LORD."

We must be able to ask such things in the same way we gratefully give thanks to God for positive experiences.

God wants us to mirror this attitude in our lives, as we reflect His values in this world.

He uses us to spread the much-needed message of salvation, to live really and truly spiritual lives, and above all to seek the Kingdom of God.

Our service for God is simply to strive for what he wants and to recognise as valuable what He deems as valuable.

We are important to God and He wants to use us.

He desires us to live in this world as he would live, if He was in our place.

God isn't bound to invest so much grace, patience and power in us, but it is His will and His heart's desire.

He could do it all alone, since He is the Creator, but He longs for communion.

It became possible for man and God to have a truly intimate relationship through His Son Jesus Christ's death and resurrection.

Jesus has already been through all that we are facing right now.

He knows the pain and rejection, our joy, feelings and thoughts.

I know them all and already took everything on himself for us.

So we can lay aside our yoke and enter into a new open court as kings and priests before Him.

God ministers to us with a father's heart.

He cares and has a vision for us.

He accompanies us, as we go along on our life's journey.

Teen Challenge has something to do with challenge.

I want to encourage us to allow ourselves to be challenged and to alig n our focus with God.

I believe with all my heart that we will experience how God's glory will become visible among the people, and the text in Isaiah 61 will become reality in our towns, streets and houses.

Everything we experience here with God is only a small harbinger of what will be in heaven.

Yet, everyone of us can already now experience a little taste of heaven.

I sense the presence of God's love and grace, which he has prepared for us, with every guest who comes to the TC Projekthof.

Our challenge consists in spirituality not only being confined to a part of our lives, but in living out our spirituality in every relationship, every feeling and every daily experience.

Teen Challenge is a missions ministry based on these spiritual principles, which has seen many lives transformed, even in Germany

Many a church or leader has found their ground through the backing and support of Teen Challenge.

The film and the book, 'The Cross and the Switchblade' by David Wilkerson, often triggers a change of course in the lives of those who come across it.

I wish Teen Challenge in Germany could again become a platform for many people and enrich the church.

Let us in this sense be followers of Jesus and not grow weary.

And please never forget where you came from, so that you know how precious life is!

The Teen Challenge Project Farm is a Christian therapy community, which is located in Walchum (in the district of Emsland), and occupies a former farm, which has been modernised and enlarged.

The establishment sees itself as an help for people who are seeking support to cope with their daily life circumstances.

The group of people comprises people who are any of the following :

a) emotionally disabled
b) at risk of emotional disability
c) drug addicts
d) troubled by life crises

On the TC Project Farm we offer intensive support for men through on-site-support in family structures with simultaneous professional integration.

The concept is based on the guidelines of Teen Challenge and includes a discipleship program to stabilize those seeking help and to restore them to a point where they can take responsibility for themselves.

We offer 12 treatment units on the farm, assisted living, day guest care and long-term life counselling.

Anybody can come to us, providing they are prepared to align their lives to God and are willing to actively cooperate in this.

We admit male guests from the age of 18 years.

No funding agency is needed!

(There are possibilities for financing of the rent and board via the employment office, social security office, grants etc.)

Vocational integration is made possible through the various branches of the farm

- Animal Husbandry
- Home Economics
- Service Provider
- Carpentry

The Carpentry is an economic operation which offers an opportunity to those seeking help from TC Project Farm to pursue practical activities and learn and develop within the therapy framework.

If the relevant requirements are fulfilled an apprenticeship as a carpenter will be offered.

Trusteeship:
The TC Project Farm (Projekthof Hasselbrock) is:
A member of the Christian Social Support Association (Arbeitsgemeinschaft christlicher Lebenshilfen (ACL)

Part of the parent organization Teen-Challenge Deutschland (Germany) e.V.

A member of Paritätischer Niedersachsen e.V.

Information and registration:
Office: Westweg 61, 26907 Walchum (Germany)
Tel.: +49 5939 1405 Fax: +49 5939 317
info@tcd-teenchallenge.de

Contact:

Bettina Rattering: +49 173 8579 540
Martin Ratering: +49 5939 1405

Information on the Internet: www.tcd-deutschland.de

Bank account Teen Challenge Germany:
Ev. Kreditgenossenschaft Frankfurt
BIC: GENODEF1EK1
IBAN: DE 47 5206 0410 0004 1137 05